GROWING
SPIRITUALLY

WITH THE

SAINTS

CATHERINE OF GENOA
WILLIAM LAW

To Pat
A Beautiful Gift From God

Reclaiming the Sacred

GROWING SPIRITUALLY WITH THE SAINTS

Catherine of Genoa
&
William Law

R. LaMon Brown

PEAKE ROAD

Macon, Georgia

ISBN 1-57312-037-5

Growing Spiritually with the Saints
Catherine of Genoa & William Law

R. LaMon Brown

Copyright © 1996

6316 Peake Road
Macon, Georgia 31210-3960
1-800-747-3016

Peake Road
is an imprint of
Smyth & Helwys Publishing, Inc.®

Library of Congress Cataloging-in-Publication Data

Brown, R. LaMon (Raymon Lamon), 1948–
    Growing spiritually with the saints:
    Catherine of Genoa & William Law / R. LaMon Brown.
    (Reclaiming the sacred)
    x + 102 pp.   6" x 9" (15 x 23 cm.)
    Includes bibliographical references.
    ISBN 1-57312-037-5 (alk. paper)
    1. Spiritual life—Christianity.
    2. Catherine, of Genoa, Saint, 1447–1510.
    3. Law, William, 1686–1761. 4. Devotional calendars.
    I. Title. II. Series.
    BV4501.2.B76674   1996   96-15753
    248.4—dc20   CIP

CONTENTS

PREFACE

Catherine of Genoa and William Law, though separated by culture and centuries, had an intense love of God. This love was manifested through years of sacrificial service. Those years of service were prepared for and strengthened by the practice of certain spiritual disciplines.

My own introduction to the disciplines began in a classroom at Golden Gate Baptist Theological Seminary. In the early 1970s, a church history professor lectured on a fourteenth-century European movement called the "Friends of God." I remember him saying these men and women were evangelical Christians before the Protestant Reformation. I was intrigued.

Some years later, still remembering the Friends of God, I took a course at New Orleans Baptist Theological Seminary on devotional classics. It introduced me more broadly to a deep river of spirituality that has run through the history of the church from Origen and Augustine to Evelyn Underhill and Henri Nouwen. A part of that spirituality is the emphasis on a disciplined lifestyle, a life that practices spiritual disciplines for the purposes of experiencing the presence of God in a more intense way and of being strengthened to lovingly obey God in all circumstances.

Two books have been influential in my own life and in the lives of many others. In *Celebration of Discipline*, Richard Foster calls us to break with the superficiality of our age and use the classical disciplines in order to live in the spiritual depths.[1] In *The Spirit of the Disciplines*, Dallas Willard urges us to arrange our lives around the same practices Jesus followed in order to have constant fellowship with God.[2]

Foster emphasizes twelve disciplines: meditation, prayer, fasting, study, simplicity, solitude, submission, service, confession, worship, guidance, and celebration. He devotes a chapter to each discipline. Willard's approach is different, but complementary. Before detailing several disciplines in chapter 9, he presents a theological and biblical basis for the disciplines. His list of disciplines includes solitude, silence, fasting, frugality, chastity, secrecy, sacrifice, study, worship, celebration, service, prayer, fellowship, confession, and submission. Neither of these lists would be inclusive of all spiritual disciplines practiced by Christians throughout history.

Another book on spirituality, *Disciplines for the Inner Life*, is structured around a devotional calendar and has fifty-two topics. While only nineteen are arranged in the section on disciplines for the inner journey, several of the other thirty-three chapters also deal with various kinds of disciplines.[3]

When I was asked to write about two saints and six disciplines illustrated in their lives, I was excited, although the task of choosing which ones was difficult. I chose Catherine because she was especially appreciated by Friedrich von Hugel who was himself a giant in the study of spirituality. I chose William Law because he was one of the few Protestants who is considered to be a part of that deep river of spirituality. Finally, I selected disciplines that were of particular importance to the two subjects and are transferable to our own lives.

Catherine's life illustrates the traditional disciplines of confession and service. The regular reception of Holy Communion was also important to her. This aspect of her spiritual life could be subsumed under the topic of worship, but I think that would be unfair to her own appreciation of the importance of Communion itself. Catherine also practiced fasting, but this was not so much something she chose as it was compelled of her.

When approaching the life of William Law, I was immediately concerned that I had already discussed the discipline of service as a part of Catherine's life. Service was an important part of Law's life as well. Nevertheless, three other disciplines were also of great importance to him: prayer, study, and simplicity or frugality.

My desire in writing this book is that God's Spirit would encourage each of us to grow in the practice of spiritual disciplines. May the examples of Catherine of Genoa and William Law be an inspiration of what God can do through lives that are committed to living in the depths rather than on the surface.

Notes

[1]Richard Foster, *Celebration of Discipline: The Path to Spiritual Growth* (New York: HarperCollins, 1978, rev. ed. 1988) 1.

[2]Dallas Willard, *The Spirit of the Disciplines: Understanding How God Changes Lives* (New York: HarperCollins, 1988) ix.

[3]Bob and Michael W. Benson, *Disciplines for the Inner Life* (Nashville: Thomas Nelson, rev. ed. 1989).

TERMINOLOGY

Examen is a way for a person to discern how God is speaking in past and present experiences. Saint Ignatius Loyola used a method of daily examen to develop in his community a discerning way of life. Noticing and becoming aware of God's presence daily requires an ongoing examining of one's life.

Lectio Divina, or divine reading, is a form of meditation, a slow, prayerful reading of the Scriptures or a passage of inspired writing. We can learn much from those persons past and present who follow this ancient practice of listening and integration. By reading the text slowly several times, word by word, and listening more carefully for the Spirit's voice, the reader enters into and is surrounded by the text. Traditionally, one monk would read a piece of scripture aloud. Silence would follow. The text would be read again, and again. When the listeners had *heard* the text, they would leave and spend time in prayer and silence.

Selah is a term that appears in the body of the psalms, and has as its root meaning "sigh" or "meditate." Some scholars say that the word refers to a pause in the singing for meditation. Others say that it is connected with rising or lifting. Still others say that the word instructed the congregation to cease singing to allow time for worshipers to show God a response or act of worship. Readers are encouraged to pause when the word "selah" appears at the end of each beginning quotation. It prepares them for a prayerful reading of what follows.

CATHERINE OF GENOA

1

DISCIPLINED
LOVER OF GOD

No more world, no more sin.[1]

Selah

Catherine was a young lady in a loveless marriage arranged by her brother for political and financial reasons. She was sixteen when she married Guiliano.[2] He was only interested in spending his family's money and having extramarital affairs. Dissolution and unfaithfulness were the marks of his personality.

During the first five years of their marriage, Catherine withdrew from the normal social life of her day. Her own family and Guiliano's were important in fifteenth-century Genoa. Social events were commonplace, but Catherine made no attempt to get involved. Largely through the urging of her family, she eventually reentered those social circles. Catherine did not, however, indulge herself in the kind of lifestyle to which her husband and others of that day seemed drawn. Her involvement in the social swirl was moderate at most. This lasted for another five years.

During the Christmas season of 1472, Catherine became severely depressed. She again withdrew from all social intercourse. On March 22, 1473, she went to a priest for the normal Lenten confession. Because of her psychological state, she was unable to make a confession. She could only kneel and ask for a blessing from the priest. As she knelt, her heart seemed pierced by the love of God. In one moment she saw her own miserable state and God's boundless love. She was so filled with contrition for sin and wonder at God's love, she almost collapsed. All she could say was "no more world, no more sin."

With these words on her lips, she returned to her home where she remained for two days. During that time she had an "inner vision."

In her imagination, she saw Jesus Christ crucified, blood from head to foot. In her mind, it was as though she heard Christ say, "This blood has been shed for your love and to atone for your sins."[3] She was filled at once with a desire to confess her sins—even publicly, if that were the Lord's will.

These combined experiences were the turning point of Catherine's life. She had repented of her sins and turned in faith to Christ. She never again turned away from God's love.

For the next four years, she practiced personal penance and mortification. The first fourteen months were the most severe. She wore a hair shirt, refused to eat food she liked, placed thorns in her bed, walked with her eyes always fixed on the ground, and prayed at least six hours each day.

She was not trying to atone for her sins; Christ had done that. She wanted, instead, to suffer for the sin by which she had offended the goodness and love of God. She was ashamed of the sin in her life that stood in stark contrast to the love of God. Although her level of mortification exceeded that of many of her contemporaries, these kinds of practices were a common feature of medieval spirituality.

During this four-year period, two very significant events took place in her husband's life: he went bankrupt, and he was converted. Catherine forgave him and seemed to have no compunction about living with him thereafter. They lived together until his death some twenty years later in 1497.

Although Guiliano was technically bankrupt, he still had a moderate income from some land he had inherited. Therefore, their choice of housing was indicative of their new religious sensibilities. In the autumn of the year of their conversions, they moved into a humble little house in a poor section of the city near the Hospital of Pammatone. Catherine began ministering to the poor. She cleaned their houses, washed their clothes, and tended their sick both in their homes and in the hospital.

In 1474, she began to receive Holy Communion daily, which was a highly unusual practice at the time. In 1476, she began to fast during the periods of Lent and Advent, although she did not choose to do this. According to biographer Friedrich von Hugel, "Her love said that

He wanted her to keep the Forty Days, in His company in the Desert."[4] For the next twenty-three years, she was scarcely able to eat anything during Lent and Advent. In spite of such austerities, her energy level seemed at its highest during the fasts.

In 1479, Catherine and Guiliano moved into two small rooms in the Pammatone Hospital, where they lived at their own expense. Catherine worked as a volunteer nurse. In 1490, she became the director of the 130-bed hospital, which also had an orphanage for 100 girls. She continued as hospital administrator until 1496 when ill health forced her to step down.

The plague struck Genoa in 1493. The experience of the Genoans was typical of medieval Europe. Most of those who could, fled the city. Of those remaining, four-fifths died of the disease.

Catherine also could have left, but she did not. She stayed and ministered to the suffering and dying. She converted the space behind the hospital into a huge open-air infirmary. Daily she could be seen moving from bed to bed offering what solace and comfort she could.

Guiliano died in 1497. Before his death, he suffered greatly. The biographers wrote that he became "very impatient."[5] Catherine was afraid that in his impatience he might do or say something that would jeopardize his salvation. With tears, she prayed that God would save him. Before Guiliano died, his "impatience" was transformed into peace.

Catherine's relationship to Guiliano, his former mistress, and his illegitimate daughter was praiseworthy. As mentioned earlier, after Guiliano's conversion, Catherine received him back into her life. Although they mutually agreed to live together celibately, no indication exists that she ever acted towards him with anything less than Christian forgiveness and charity. When she became aware of his former mistress and illegitimate daughter, she responded in like manner. She was always solicitous for their welfare. An indication of this concern is found in one of her wills where she bequeathed to the daughter Tobias (then a grown woman) her favorite silk robe.

Another important year for Catherine was 1499. Her great fasts ended, and she accepted her first spiritual director/confessor. He was Don Cattaneo Marabotto, her succesor as director of the hospital.

During the latter years of her life, Catherine found time to speak to others about her interior life and spiritual understanding. From this period come most of the sayings attributed to her in her biography and in *Purgation and Purgatory* and *The Spiritual Dialogue.*

Also from this period we have the first glimpses that her love for God and for other persons extended to nature and animals as well. Her heart would break at the death of any animal. During her last painful years, she would request the window in her room to be opened so that she might see the beauty of the sky.

It is difficult to know exactly when Catherine's health began to fail. Some point to 1501; others to 1506. In spite of her illness, she continued, even after 1506, to actively serve the hospital and minister to the orphans.

Nevertheless, her physical condition continued to decline. Her doctors assumed her illness was caused by supernatural forces. Modern students of her life suggest her symptoms may point to a kidney disease. The end finally came on Sunday, September 15, 1510.

Catherine's life and thought are worthy of examination. She was a married laywoman. She was a mystic and a humanitarian. She was a contemplative who always remained active in ministering to the sick and destitute. Her life was marked by years of taxing labor, but she never seemed to lose her sense of God's present love.

She went about the business of the hospital with her heart so filled with joy that inwardly she would recite rhymes of love to God. The following is a translation of one:

> Dost thou wish that I should show
> All God's Being thou mayst know?
> Peace is not found in those who do not with Him go.[6]

What could cause such a response to God in the life of an administrator? Rightly or wrongly, the word "administrator" conjures up the picture of a serious, disciplined sort of person. I would dare say that the desire to spontaneously recite joyful rhymes of love to God is not normally associated with the administrative character. Catherine was, however, a good administrator. She took a hands-on approach to running the hospital. Her financial books were always balanced.

How did she escape the danger of being so immersed in the details of hospital management that she would forget the joy of the Lord? On the divine side, she received the blessings of God's grace. On the human side, she practiced certain disciplines or spiritual activities that enabled her to know joy and peace. Three of these disciplines, confession, Holy Communion, and service, will be examined in the following chapters.

Lectio Divina

Now the Lord is the Spirit, and where the Spirit of the Lord is, there is freedom. And all of us, with unveiled faces, seeing the glory of the Lord as though reflected in a mirror, are being transformed into the same image from one degree of glory to another; for this comes from the Lord, the Spirit. (2 Cor 3:17-18)

Examen

Today take time to reflect on two events in your life. Remember the time when you first remember knowing the presence of God or Christ. In evangelical circles, this is usually one's conversion experience. Then recall another experience of God's loving presence in later years. Allow the realities of these experiences to renew your heart and move you to that next "degree of glory."

Prayer

Lord Jesus, thank you for your presence in my life. You revealed yourself to the early disciples. You revealed yourself to Paul. You revealed yourself to Catherine. You revealed yourself to me. I thank you for revealing yourself with voices and visions to some. I do not claim these, but I rejoice that your revelation to me is no less real. Your spirit dwells in me, and I am free. All praise to your name. Amen.

Notes

[1]Catherine of Genoa, quoted in Benedict J. Groeschel, "The Spiritual Dialogue," *Catherine of Genoa: Purgation and Purgatory, The Spiritual Dialogue*, Serge Hughes, trans. (New York: Paulist Press, 1979) 109.

[2]Groeschel, "Introduction," 3. (Unless otherwise noted, all such material is found here or in Friedrich von Hugel, *The Mystical Element of Religion as Studied in Saint Catherine of Genoa and Her Friends*.)

[3]Catherine, *The Spiritual Dialogue*, 118.

[4]Friedrich von Hugel, *The Mystical Element of Religion as Studied in Saint Catherine of Genoa and Her Friends*, 2 vols. (London: J. M. Dent & Sons Ltd., 1908) 1:135.

[5]Ibid., 1:150.

[6]Evelyn Underhill, *Mysticism: A Study in the Nature and Development of Man's Spiritual Consciousness*, 3rd ed. (London: Methuen & Co., 1930; New York: E. P. Dutton & Co., 1955) 441.

≈2≈

CONFESSION

Never excuse thyself, but always be ready to accuse thyself.[1]

Selah

In chapter 1, we discussed Catherine's life-changing experiences around the age of twenty-six. Primary sources[2] tell us Catherine was despondent after ten years in a loveless, degrading marriage. Her sister encouraged her to go to a confession during the Lenten season. She went, but was unable to confess. God made her

> understand the extent of her ingratitude and mirrored herself in her sins; and she was overcome with such despair and self-loathing that she was tempted to publicly confess her sins. And Catherine's soul cried out, "O Lord, no more world, no more sins!"[3]

Returning to her home, she spent the next two days in agony.

> Catherine was sick with heartache, unshed tears and sighs, sick unto death. She could not eat, sleep, or talk, nor had she any taste for things, either spiritual or earthly. She had no sense of where she was, in heaven or on earth, and would gladly have hidden from everyone. So alienated was she by the offense given to God that she looked more like a frightened animal than a human being. The pain of enduring that vision of sin was as keen-edged and hard as a diamond.

When God had her dwell on that vision, however, God then provided for her in the following way:

> One day there appeared to her inner vision Jesus Christ incarnate crucified, all bloody from head to foot. It seemed the body rained blood. From within she heard a voice say, "Do you see this blood? It has been shed for your love, to atone for your sins." With that she received a wound of love that drew her to Jesus.[4]

Although this experience was the turning point of her life, she still had some turning to do.

> She was granted another vision. . . . God showed her the love with which He had suffered out of love for her. . . . In that vision, Catherine [also] saw the evil in the soul and the purity of God's love. The two never left her. Had she dwelt on that vision any longer than she did, she would have fainted, become undone. . . .
>
> In turning her gaze upon herself, Catherine saw how much evil there was in her. She waged resolute war on the self-love that survived in her. . . .
>
> Still trusting in God, she said: "Lord, I make you a present of myself. I do not know what to do with myself. Let me, then Lord, make this exchange: I will place this evil being into your hands. You're are the only one who can hide it in your goodness . . . On your part, you will grant your pure love, which will extinguish all other loves in me and will annihilate me and busy me so much with you that I will have no time or place for anything or anyone else."
>
> The Lord accepted. As a consequence, these preoccupations never troubled Catherine again.[5]

This does not mean Catherine never again felt her own imperfections in the light of God's perfect love. Rather, an emotional outpouring of sorrow over sin never again impeded her more normal duties.

Her biographers emphasize that Catherine's sorrow was not for any obvious moral transgression. By all accounts, she was the opposite of her profligate husband in his pre-conversion days. Sorrow burned in her heart because, compared to the pure love of God shown in the cross of Christ, her own soul appeared ingratious and hateful. She repented in tears, not because she had lied or cheated or stolen or murdered. She repented because she had, in one degree or another, ignored that pure, unselfish love. Faced with a vision of God's love, any degree of neglect was abhorrent to her.

Catherine continued to develop the discipline of confession on her own, although others encouraged her to adopt a spiritual director or confessor, as was the practice of Catholics of her day. But the Lord spoke to her otherwise: "Confide in me and doubt not."[6] This situation lasted for twenty-five years. About eleven years before her death, however, Catherine accepted as her director/confessor the new hospital administrator, Dom Cattaneo Marabotto. Her first confession to him was similar to those that regularly followed. She said, "I would like to confess, but I cannot perceive any offence committed by me."[7]

Marabotto was able to encourage and comfort her during the painful trials that lay ahead, but no human confessor seemed able to draw from her a confession of sin. That confession came only when faced with the pure love of God. Catherine said,

> When from time to time I would advert to the matter, it seemed to me that my love was complete; but later as time went on and as my sight. . . . These things are clearly visible in the mirror of truth, that is of Pure Love, where everything is seen crooked which before appeared straight.[8]

In her last months, she had another vision:

> She saw many of the wretched parts of her life, and that greatly distressed her. When she could speak of them she did, and then the distress left her. They were things of no importance, but for her the least defect was intolerable.[9]

Christians have always looked on confession of sins as a necessary part of the Christian life. References to confession are found throughout the New Testament. The very first paragraph of the Gospel of Mark records that those people who were preparing for the coming of the Messiah responded to the message of John the Baptist by confessing their sins and being baptized (1:1-5).

Although he did not use the word "confession," Paul's affirmation of his own unworthiness to be an apostle involved the confession of sin, specifically of persecuting the church (cf. 1 Cor 15:9; 1 Tim 1:15). Romans 7:13-24 is another confession of the problem of sin in Paul's life.

Catherine confessed her sin. Through these times of confession, she grew spiritually. If we want to grow likewise, we must practice the discipline of confession.

11

In *Prayer: Finding the Hearts True Home*, Richard Foster devotes one chapter to the Prayer of Examen.[10] This prayer is the attempt to accurately evaluate one's situation. It has two elements: (1) It reflects on how God has been with us during the day, and (2) it examines our conscience to see what needs cleansing and forgiving. The latter is our concern here.

Confession is not intended to tear open our souls as a whip ripping into the back of a condemned criminal. Pain is a part of confession, but it is neither masochistic on our part not sadistic on God's.

In the discipline of confession, we humbly ask God to reveal to us how we truly are. Catherine's periods of confession were times of comparison. God granted her to see her life compared to God's. Next to God's love and graciousness, Catherine's life seemed cold and entirely lacking in gratitude. In those moments of grace, Catherine was stirred to confess—not so much sins of commission, but sins of omission or faults in her very character. With the confession came God's gift of peace and forgiveness. These gifts helped Catherine to grow.

Let me suggest three means for experiencing this discipline and this grace. These ideas are certainly not new. They have proved their worth in the lives of many saints who wanted to grow more like God.

(1) *Read the Ten Commandments*. Read them slowly and prayerfully. Read them asking God to reveal to you your own failures. Pause after each commandment to allow God to bring to your mind any failures or omissions in your life that need to be forgiven and corrected.

(2) *Pray the Lord's Prayer with confession in mind*. I can remember times when one phrase or another led me into confession. "Hallowed be your name"; forgive me Lord, for I have gone a whole day without any praise of you on my lips. "Your will be done"; forgive me Lord for caring far too much about my wants and not enough about yours. I could go on, but you get the picture.

(3) *Read a story about Jesus from the Gospels*. Almost any story will do. In this reading, you are not trying to understand every nuance or detail. Don't get bogged down in minutiae. Read the story to learn

12

again what Jesus was like. Read it to compare your life with his. Pray that God will lead you into the right confession.

In writing about these three methods, I was thinking primarily about private confession between an individual and God. It is possible these could be used in a small group setting as well—which brings us to the matter of confession to someone other than God.

Catherine used a confessor the last years of her life. In the New Testament, James encouraged his readers to confess to one another. It is interesting, but perhaps not surprising, that in their books on Christian discipline, both Dallas Willard and Richard Foster deal with the discipline of confession as a corporate discipline.[11] According to Willard,

> Confession is a discipline that functions within fellowship. In it we let trusted others know our deepest weaknesses and failures. This will nourish our faith in God's provision for our needs through his people, our sense of being loved, and our humility before our brothers and sisters.[12]

Recently the importance of this aspect of confession became evident to me. In a conversation with a trusted Christian friend, I talked about my feelings of frustration and inadequacy related to the pastoral ministry. My friend helped me to see more clearly that, although these feelings reflected some of the reality in my life, they were not the whole story. Encouraged, I was better prepared to face changes in my ministerial situation that, unbeknown to me, were about to occur. I suspect Catherine's confessor was able to offer her similar words of encouragement and hope.

Lectio Divina

If we confess our sins, he who is faithful and just will forgive us our sins and cleanse us from all unrighteousness. (1 John 1:9)

Therefore confess your sins to one another, and pray for one another, so that you may be healed. (Jas 5:16a)

13

Examen

Examine your life for the past few days. Confess any transgressions of God's commandments. Confess any failures on your part to live up to the commandments of Christ to love God and neighbor. Confess any feelings or attitudes in your life that are unworthy of one who seeks to be like Jesus. Ask God to reveal to you the name of someone with whom you could confess your needs.

Prayer

Our Father in heaven, hallowed be your name. Your kingdom come. Your will be done, on earth as it is in heaven. Give us this day our daily bread. And forgive us our debts, as we also have forgiven our debtors. And do not bring us to the time of trial, but rescue us from the evil one. (Matt 6:9-13)

Notes

[1]Catherine of Genoa, quoted in Benedict J. Groeschel, "Introduction," *Catherine of Genoa: Purgation and Purgatory, The Spiritual Dialogue*, Serge Hughes, trans. (New York: Paulist Press, 1979) 13.

[2]For primary sources on the life of Catherine, see *Life and Doctrine of Saint Catherine of Genoa, Purgation and Purgatory* (or more traditionally, *Treatise on Purgatory*), and *The Spiritual Dialogue*. *Life and Doctrine* has long been out of print, but the salient points of her life are found in the other two works. None of these works were written directly by Catherine; they are the remembrances of her disciples and friends.

[3]Catherine, *The Spiritual Dialogue*, 109.

[4]Ibid., 117-18.

[5]Ibid., 118-19.

[6]Friedrich von Hugel, *The Mystical Element of Religion as Studied in Saint Catherine of Genoa and Her Friends*, 2 vols. (London: J. M. Dent & Sons Ltd., 1908) 1:117.

[7]Ibid., 1:158.

[8]Ibid., 1:267.

[9]Catherine, *The Spiritual Dialogue*, 146.

[10]Richard Foster, *Prayer: Finding the Heart's True Home* (New York: HarperCollins, 1992) 27-35.

[11]Richard Foster, *Celebration of Discipline: The Path to Spiritual Growth* (New York: HarperCollins, 1978, rev. ed. 1988) 143-57; Dallas Willard, *The Spirit of the Disciplines: Understanding How God Changes Lives* (New York: HarperCollins, 1988) 187-89.

[12]Willard, 187.

3

HOLY COMMUNION

Now swiftly, swiftly convey it to the heart, since it is the heart's true food.[1]

Selah

Beginning in May 1474—a little more than a year after her conversion—and continuing until her death, Catherine began to receive Holy Communion on a daily basis. While the daily reception of the Eucharist became more popular in later centuries, it was very unusual in the fifteenth century.

Catherine had made a resolve to turn against self and to translate love into deeds.

> In that resolve, the ray of God so united her to Him that from this time on no force or passion would separate them from one another. In witness of this union, some three days later . . . she felt the pull of Holy Communion, which from that day on never left her.[2]

In all of her writings, Catherine never developed a eucharistic doctrine. We cannot be sure what was involved in her thinking related to Holy Communion, but she never talked about it as a renewing of the sacrifice of Christ or as a source of her salvation.

The quote at the opening of this chapter indicates that her normal desire was to interiorize the Eucharist. The word "heart" must not be taken to imply that she was primarily interested in an emotional experience, however. From *The Spiritual Dialogue* comes the following story.

"Human Frailty" was despondent because the "Soul" was leading it more and more into spiritual matters. Human Frailty went to church, received Communion, and was so illuminated that like the Soul it felt it was already enjoying eternal bliss. However, the Soul was not pleased. Human Frailty was finding joy in feelings rather than in Pure Love or God. Soul thus prayed,

Lord, Lord, I want no signs from you, nor am I looking for intense feelings to accompany your love. I would rather flee those feelings as I do the devil. They get in the way of Pure Love—for under the guise of Pure Love it is those emotional feelings to which the soul becomes attached. . . . A spiritual attachment that seems good is dangerous: It can mislead the Soul into attaching itself not to God but to those pleasurable sentiments.[3]

Catherine's taking of Communion did not unite her with God; that union had already taken place. She took Communion daily, but not just to experience an emotional joy. Nor did she feel a need to take Communion in order to be assured of her salvation. She took it as a token or "witness" that she was with God and God was with her. Although she did not write a doctrine of the Eucharist, it seems clear that Holy Communion was an important part of her spiritual growth and life. Several modern writers have emphasized how important it can be for us as well.

Growing up in a Baptist church, I do not remember any real attachment to the Lord's Supper, as we called it. Our church observed it about once a quarter. It seemed to be tacked on to the end of the service without any serious attention given to explaining that, even if it were "only a sign," it was nevertheless filled with significance. In defense of my home church and those early pastors, as a young person I probably did not listen too carefully to what they said anyway!

Having been a pastor, a missionary, and an occasional visitor in non-Baptist services, I have developed a better understanding of how important the Eucharist can be in the life of every believer. Richard Foster expresses it well:

At the heart of all Christian prayer is the celebration of the Eucharist, or Holy Communion. Nearly every aspect of prayer is caught up in the eucharistic feast: examination, repentance, petition, forgiveness, contemplation, thanksgiving, celebration, and more. It most perfectly embodies the central core of prayer in that we are full participants in the action, but the grace that comes is all of God. All the senses are employed. We see, we smell, we touch, we taste. We hear the words of institution: "This is my body. . . . This is my blood." In short, Eucharistic Prayer is the most complete prayer we ever make this side of eternity.[4]

I do not remember all of that being involved in my church's practice of Communion, but those times when I have received Communion in this way, it has been a marvelous and strengthening experience.

In addition to the prayer aspect of Communion, the service itself faithfully reminds us that the sacrifice of Christ is at the heart of the gospel. In that remembrance, our faith is nourished, and our love grows.

Am I recommending Catherine's practice of daily Communion? I do not practice it myself, but here is the account of someone who does. Morton Kelsey wrote of his and his wife's experience:

> At her suggestion we began to celebrate Eucharist daily together. This has brought us together both spiritually and emotionally. I experience Eucharist, the most ancient and central Christian way of worship, as complete prayer, embracing all elements of communion with God. In it we come quietly into God's presence, we confess our failures, receive absolution, meditatively listen to scripture, let ourselves go in adoration, live through the ritual that Jesus gave us before he was betrayed and crucified, have fellowship with the risen Jesus, commune with God, offer thanksgiving, and receive God's blessing. This daily ritual has added another dimension, a great depth, to our life of fellowship with God. We have found that we can celebrate Eucharist wherever we go—in motel rooms and in airports, as well as in our home or in a church. God is not confined to church buildings.[5]

Some of you may be suspicious of this emphasis on the Eucharist. You may fear that it will lead to a misunderstanding about how one is saved. You may be nervous that such a regular act could devolve into rote ritual without any real meaning. You also may have reservations about taking Communion outside the context of a local church fellowship.

I want us to widen our perspective at this point. Whether one adopts Catherine's practice or not, there is, nonetheless, a principle of spiritual growth involved that is crucial to us all.

Friedrich von Hugel wrote about the three elements in religion.[6] He used various terms to identify the areas. The first he calls historical, traditional, institutional. The second is thinking, analysis, philosophic. The third is intuitive, emotional, volitional.

One might debate von Hugel's terminology and perhaps other aspects of his discussion, but I am convinced that healthy religion needs the traditional, institutional side as much as it needs the other two. We need this side of religion in order to safeguard our moorings. Without it we could wander in the nether regions of the intellect and espouse speculative ideas without any basis for evaluation. Without it we would be more subject to the whims of our emotions and volition to carry us to places we should not go.

Christianity without an authoritative, traditional, and institutional side is like a boat without an anchor: it is in danger. (Of course, an anchor without a boat is of little use either. All three elements are important.)

Catherine fed this aspect of her religious life through daily reception of the Eucharist and regular readings from the Bible and other spiritual books. Perhaps daily Communion is not for you, but the disciplines of traditional church services are of vital importance.

Both Dallas Willard and Richard Foster talk about the disciplines of study, worship, and celebration.[7] In my Baptist upbringing, daily Bible reading and weekly church attendance were expected. This is a part of the institutional side of religion of which von Hugel wrote. I cannot say enough about how important both were and continue to be to my spiritual growth.

In light of Catherine's practice, von Hugel's analysis, and Willard and Foster's emphases, let me suggest three courses of action that may help in spiritual growth.

First, do not ignore regular corporate worship in the pursuit of something more "spiritual." Jesus went regularly to the synagogue (Luke 4:16). The writer of Hebrews urged his readers to "provoke one another to love and good deeds, not neglecting to meet together, as is the habit of some" (Heb 10:24-25). Following the tradition of meeting together at least once a week for corporate prayer and worship is a basic building block for anyone who wants to be spiritually sound.

Second, take Communion seriously and often. "Often" is, of course, a relative word. In most of the churches I have been a part of for the last ten years, we have observed the Lord's Supper monthly. I have found that to be helpful. Occasionally I have attended an early morning Episcopal service just to participate in the Eucharist. If your church takes Communion too infrequently for the discipline to really take hold in your life, encourage an increased number of observances, and look for other opportunities to take Communion.

As I indicated, I do not take Communion daily. I also have never taken it outside of a corporate setting, but I may someday. Others have found it to be helpful. As a possible substitute for daily Communion, however, let me make my third suggestion.

Read the Passion stories regularly. Read them silently. Read them aloud. Read them slowly and reverently. Visualize as you read. See Jesus dying on a cross for you. I have a tendency to want to quickly move on to the resurrection. We must first allow the reality of the cross to seep into our minds and hearts.

Reading the Passion stories does not remove the need for Communion, but many of the elements of Communion may be found in this kind of prayerful, spiritual reading. We are moved to confession, thanksgiving, and celebration.

Lectio Divina

For I received from the Lord what I also handed on to you, that the Lord Jesus on the night when he was betrayed took a loaf of bread, and when he had given thanks, he broke it and said, "This is my body that is for you. Do this in remembrance of me." In the same way he took the cup also, after supper, saying, "This cup is the new covenant in my blood. Do this, as often as you drink it, in remembrance of me." For as often as you eat this bread and drink this cup, you proclaim the Lord's death until he comes. (1 Cor 11:23-26)

The cup of blessing that we bless, is it not a sharing in the blood of Christ? The bread that we break, is it not a sharing in the body of Christ? (1 Cor 10:16)

Examen

Reflect on your past participation in the institutional side of the religious life. How committed have you been to regular, corporate worship? How seriously have you partaken of Holy Communion? Ask God to strengthen this part of your life.

Prayer

> *Lord Jesus, you are the head of the Body, the church. Thank you for drawing me into that holiest of institutions. Lord Jesus, you are the present glory in Holy Communion. As I participate in the Lord's Supper, may my faith in your daily lordship be strengthened. Lord Jesus, for these gifts, I thank you. Make me worthy to receive them. In your name. Amen.*

Notes

[1] Friedrich von Hugel, *The Mystical Element of Religion as Studied in Saint Catherine of Genoa and Her Friends*, 2 vols. (London: J. M. Dent & Sons Ltd., 1908) 1:115.

[2] Catherine of Genoa, quoted in Benedict J. Groeschel, "The Spiritual Dialogue," *Catherine of Genoa: Purgation and Purgatory, The Spiritual Dialogue*, Serge Hughes, trans. (New York: Paulist Press, 1979) 110.

[3] Ibid., 122-24.

[4] Richard Foster, *Prayer: Finding the Heart's True Home* (New York: HarperCollins, 1992) 111.

[5] Morton Kelsey, *Reaching: The Journey to Fulfillment* (San Francisco: Harper & Row, 1989; Minneapolis MN: Augsburg, 1994) 79.

[6] Von Hugel, 1:50-82.

[7] Richard Foster, *Celebration of Discipline: The Path to Spiritual Growth* (New York: HarperCollins, 1978, rev. ed. 1988) 62-75, 143-57, 190-201; Dallas Willard, *The Spirit of the Disciplines: Understanding How God Changes Lives* (New York: HarperCollins, 1988) 176-81.

4

SERVICE

"Thou commandest me to love my neighbor," she complained to her Love, "and yet I cannot love anything but Thee, nor can I admit of anything else, and mix it up with Thee. How, then shall I act?" And she received the interior answer: "He who loves me, loves all that I love."[1]

Selah

After her conversion, Catherine became a servant. She volunteered to clean the houses of the poor, wash their clothes, and tend their sick so they might be free to find work of their own. Before becoming a hospital administrator, she worked for years as a volunteer nurse. Even in her hospital job during the plague years, she continued to minister to the needs of the sick and dying patients.

A beautiful story is told concerning those terrible times. A devout woman was dying of the plague in the open-air ward behind the hospital. For eight days she lay in speechless agony. Catherine visited her every day and encouraged her to call on Jesus. The woman could not speak, but she moved her lips in an attempt to speak the name of Jesus. Catherine was so overcome with compassion that she kissed the woman's parched, dying lips.[2] In this act, she modeled Jesus' loving touch of frightful lepers.

The story of Argentina del Sale is another example of Catherine's willingness to serve.[3] We do not know exactly how Catherine and Angentina first knew one another. Argentina may have been an occasional day servant for Catherine. After Argentina married a poor man named Marco del Sale, Catherine did not see her again for a year.

One day Argentina went to the hospital to see Catherine. Marco was dying. He was suffering in terrible pain with cancer of the face. The hopelessness of his situation, coupled with his physical agony, had made Marco delirious. Catherine went immediately with Argentina.

She eased his mental agony with words of comfort. She also spent time in a nearby chapel praying for him. Marco was not healed, but he experienced a profound peace from her visit and prayers.

Some time later he asked his wife to bring Catherine back. When she went to his room, he thanked her for what she had done and requested one more favor. He asked Catherine if she would care for Argentina after his death. She gladly agreed to do so. After Marco died, Argentina went to live with Catherine as her spiritual daughter.

Catherine's service to the sick and dying was an inspiration to many people, but perhaps none so much as Ettore Vernazza, a Genoese notary from an influential family. Ettore became a spiritual son to Catherine. He began to serve the sick. He gave all of his wealth to care for the poor and founded a number of institutions for them, the most famous of which was the Oratory of Divine Love. Prior to his death from the plague in 1524, through Ettore, the influence of Catherine had spread beyond the borders of her Genoa.[4]

Catherine's servant nature was also demonstrated in her preparation for death. Throughout her last painful years, Catherine prepared several wills. Each one made generous provision for orphans and others living in poverty.

The discipline of service did not come easy for Catherine. So, if it does not come easy to us, we may take heart. Catherine became a great servant in spite of two aspects of her character: her fastidiousness and her desire to focus only on God. She had come from a wealthy, influential family. She was not used to being around filth and desease. She realized that in order to serve others the way God wanted her to, she needed to overcome her inbred squeamishness.

I hesitate to mention the specifics for fear that some readers of this account would immediately write Catherine off as some kind of bizarre pervert. What she did, however, she did only at the beginning of her Christian life. While it seemed to help her, she never recommended these activities for others. In order to overcome her aversion to the sick, Catherine ate lice, touched sores with her mouth, and rubbed her nose in pus. Through these actions, "Catherine was heartened in her resolve to help the desperately sick."[5]

If we are to minister to the suffering in our day, we will need to overcome our own fear and disgust at the deformity and frightfulness of poverty and disease. I do not recommend Catherine's extreme measures, but through perserverance and prayer we can conquer our fears. Like Catherine, we will be able to embrace those who are suffering.

In addition to overcoming her oversensitivity and disgust toward negative conditions, Catherine had to overcome her desire to focus solely on God. "She was very drawn to solitude, to God Himself alone; and God gave her the gift of prayer, so that she would be on her knees for six or seven hours."[6]

Her desire for solitude with God was evident even at an early age. When she was thirteen, Catherine requested entrance into an Augustinian convent. Because of her age, she was refused. It is interesting that in her adult years, she never sought to join a convent. But she still desired to be alone with God.

Catherine's struggle is not unique in Christian history. Christians have sought solitude for centuries. Jesus spent hours and hours alone with his Father (cf. Matt 14:23; Luke 5:15; 6:12). Paul's reference of going to Arabia (Gal 1:17) is often understood as a time of solitude with God. The prayer of Thomas á Kempis expresses the sentiments of contemplatives throughout the centuries:

> O my God, when will silence, retirement, and prayer become the occupations of my soul as they are now frequently the objects of my desires.[7]

Indeed, solitude and prayer are important disciplines for the Christian life, but Jesus reminds us that love of God and love of neighbor must go together (Matt 22:36-39). Catherine struggled with this spiritual reality. The opening quote in this chapter is indicative of her inner conflict. She wanted to love God and God alone. But God reminded her that to love God truly, one must love what God loves. God loves the world. God loves the orphans and widows. God loves those who are suffering.

In one section of her *Spiritual Dialogue*, the two problems in her life seem to come together. "Human Frailty"—a part of Catherine's character—becomes willing to serve the sick, but requests a love that would impel her to that work. She said, "To do the work well, love is needed." Therefore God gave her "a certain corresponding love." Then when Catherine was put in charge of the hospital, she was "strengthened in her work by an increase of love."[8]

Catherine never abandoned her hours of prayer. She loved being alone with God. She would refuse to answer calls of curiosity. If, however, the call was to service, she would respond immediately.[9] She achieved a life in which contemplation and action balanced one another.

Just as Catherine certainly found support in the life of Jesus for her emphasis on prayer and solitude, so she found support for her life of service. Jesus was famous throughout Galilee and Judea for his ministry to the sick and displaced of society. He served them diligently, tirelessly. Perhaps, however, if one asks about Jesus and service, the story of John 13:1-17 comes to mind. Jesus washed his disciples' dirty feet as an act of service *and* as an example of service. Likewise, we are to be servants.

Specifically how we are to serve depends on our individual circumstances and abilities. The following is a very eclectic list of service possibilities. The order is entirely arbitrary.

(1) Volunteer to work in a hospital, nursing home, or homeless shelter. "Volunteer" is the key. If you are paid for the service, it may still be a wonderful help, but it is not the discipline of service as practiced by Christians for centuries.
(2) Visit the elderly and shut-ins in your community.
(3) Get involved in programs where you can be a father, mother, big brother, or big sister for some disadvantaged child.
(4) Promote and get involved in programs to make your community more beautiful and safe.
(5) Encourage your elected officials to support programs that minister to the needs of the poor, the elderly, and the sick.
(6) Serve the environment by refusing to pollute the air, the land, or the waters. Remember, to love God is to love what God loves. God is the creator of nature. The discipline of service includes environmental concerns.

(7) Practice each day small acts of service. For example, call a sick neighbor, write an encouraging note to a family member, babysit for a friend while he or she buys groceries, donate good clothing or food to a charitable organization.

Although Jesus calls Christians to a life of service, the discipline of service carries with itself a particular danger: the danger of thinking we must meet every need we see. The fact is we cannot, and we are not expected to. To try to do everything is a certain recipe for doing nothing well and eventually, out of despair, doing nothing at all.

Thomas Kelly understood that the world is too vast and one lifetime is too short for any one person to try to shoulder all responsibilities. He wrote,

> [God] does not burden us equally with all things, but considerately puts upon each of us just a few central tasks, as emphatic responsibilities. For each of these special undertakings are our share in the joyous burdens of love. . . . In the foreground is the special task, uniquely illuminated, toward which we feel a special yearning and care. . . . But in the background is a second level, or layer, of universal concern for all the multitude of good things that need doing. Toward them all we feel kindly, but we are dismissed from active service in most of them. And we have an easy mind in the presence of desperately real needs which are not our direct responsibility. We cannot die on every cross, nor are we expected to.[10]

Pray everyday that God will bring to you opportunities of service. Pray everyday that God will give you the wisdom to know what you should and should not do.

Lectio Divina

> *Let mutual love continue. Do not neglect to show hospitality to strangers, for by doing that some have entertained angels without knowing it. Remember those who are in prison, as though you were in prison with them; those who are being tortured, as though you yourselves were being tortured. . . .*

29

Therefore Jesus also suffered outside the city gate in order to sanctify the people by his own blood. Let us then go to him outside the camp and bear the abuse he endured. For here we have no lasting city, but we are looking for the city that is to come. Through him, then, let us continually offer a sacrifice of praise to God, that is, the fruit of lips that confess his name. Do not neglect to do good and to share what you have, for such sacrifices are pleasing to God. (Heb 13:1-3, 12-16)

Examen

How have you served other persons this week? What opportunities of service that you could have performed were left undone? Spend some time in prayer asking God to help you have a servant's heart and to open your eyes to service opportunities around you.

Prayer

O Father who so loved the world that you gave your only Son; O Jesus who came not to be served, but to serve; O Holy Spirit who has come to serve the name of Jesus, transform me, triune God, into a servant who is pleasing to God, imaging the Lord, and lead by the Spirit. In the name of the one who is holy, holy, holy. Amen.

Notes

[1]Friedrich von Hugel, *The Mystical Element of Religion as Studied in Saint Catherine of Genoa and Her Friends*, 2 vols. (London: J. M. Dent & Sons Ltd., 1908) 1:280.

[2]Benedict J. Groeschel, "Introduction," *Catherine of Genoa: Purgation and Purgatory, The Spiritual Dialogue*, Serge Hughes, trans. (New York: Paulist Press, 1979) 15.

[3]Von Hugel, 1:169-71.

[4]Groeschel, 15.

[5]Catherine, The *Spiritual Dialogue*, 131.

[6]Ibid., 120.

[7]Thomas á Kempis, quoted by Bob Benson and Michael Benson, *Disciplines for the Inner Life* (Nashville TN: Thomas Nelson, 1989) 59.

[8]Catherine, *The Spiritual Dialogue*, 132.

[9]Von Hugel, 1:139-40.

[10]Thomas Kelly, quoted by Benson and Benson, 340-41.

❧5❧

MEDITATIONS

Day One

The soul that has but the slightest imperfection would rather throw itself into a thousand hells than appear thus before the divine presence.[1]

Selah

Catherine believed that a person who had begun to receive the grace of God would be increasingly disturbed by the difference between God's purity and that person's uncleanness. The closer a person gets to God, the more aware of his or her sin the person becomes. That was Catherine's experience, and it has been born out in almost every revival service I have ever been a part of. More often than not, those who come in repentence and rededication are those who are already loving and serving God.

I don't know how close to God Peter and Isaiah were when they came face to face with the Divine, but their response was indicative of one who knew God and one's own self. Let's reflect on their stories and how they may correspond to our own spirituality.

Peter's story is found in Luke 5:1-9. Peter and Andrew, James and John were fishermen. They were cleaning their nets after a night of fruitless fishing. Jesus asked Peter to put his boat back into the water a bit so that Jesus could teach the crowds along the shore. After teaching, Jesus told Peter to go out into the deep and let down his nets to catch some fish. Peter seemed a bit incredulous, but agreed to do it since a teacher had asked him. The catch startled everyone. It was so large that the nets of two boats were scarcely enough to bring it in. Peter saw Jesus in a new light. "Go away from me Lord, for I am a sinful man," he said. Awe and fear colored his words.

Isaiah's experience (Isa 6) was certainly more exotic than Peter's. He saw strange heavenly beings called seraphs. He saw the temple filling with smoke. He heard voices calling out, "Holy, holy, holy is the LORD of hosts; the whole earth is full of his glory." As amazing as those things were, they paled in significance to the centerpiece of the vision. Isaiah saw the Lord "sitting on a throne, high and lofty." Isaiah's response? "Woe is me! I am lost, for I am a man of unclean lips."

Lectio Divina

> *To you I lift up my eyes, O you who are entrhoned in the heavens! As the eyes of servants look to the hand of their master, as the eyes of a maid to the hand of her mistress, so our eyes look to the LORD our God, until he has mercy upon us. Have mercy upon us, O LORD. (Ps 123:1-3a)*

Examen

The stories of Peter and Isaiah go beyond their declarations of sin, but it may be good for us to stop there and let God speak to us. Maybe you will want to choose one of those stories and meditate further on it. Place yourself in the role of Peter or Isaiah. See the story unfold before you. Feel the awe and fear. Know that in seeing God, our own selves are illuminated.

Prayer

> *Almighty and holy God, you are full of beauty, truth, and goodness. Steadfast love and compassion are ever with you. Your glory permeates my world, my life. In the light of your glory, in the light of the face of Jesus, I confess that I am a sinner. I do not obey as Jesus obeyed. I do not love as Jesus loves. I am unworthy to be called a child of God or a follower of Christ. I ask for your mercy and forgiveness. Thank you for helping me to see myself in the light of your purity. Thank you for the promise that I will be like you, all light and love and holiness. Amen*

Day Two

If a man would see properly in spiritual matters, let him pluck out the eye of his own presumption.[2]

Selah

Presumption was the middle name of Saul of Tarsus. Saul was a very religious person. He had studied under one of the greatest teachers of his day. He had joined the strictest Jewish sect. He had scrupulously obeyed the law of God as it was interpreted in his day. He had been quick to denounce all heretics, especially those who claimed that Jesus of Nazareth was the Messiah.

Somewhere on the road to Damascus, Paul had his eye of presumption plucked out. Or to be more literal, he was blinded by the light of the Messiah whose name was Jesus. The story is recorded in Acts 9. After that painful and wonderful experience of reconstructive vision enhancement, Paul became one of the most effective proclaimers of the gospel the church has ever had.

Paul's problem was not that he was wrong about everything. In fact, he was right about most things. He believed in the one creator God who had called Abraham to be the father of the people of Israel. He believed that God's commandments revealed to Moses were to be unquestioningly obeyed. He believed that Israel had been chosen in some wonderful way to be the womb of the promised Messiah. Because he was right about so much, perhaps Paul forgot that he could also be wrong.

The Scripture teaches that pride goes before a fall. A person filled with presumption is like an ice hockey player who has tripped and is sliding out of control. Both will eventually hit a wall. For Paul, the wall was on the road to Damascus. One of my walls was in a classroom at Serampore College in India.

I was a recent seminary graduate, newly arrived on the mission field, teaching my first course in theology. I did a great job. Any university or seminary in America would have been satisfied to have had their students receive such teaching. But I wasn't in America. As the course gradually unfolded and the term drew to a close, I came to realize that I had failed. God, in God's grace, may have given me a D, but I gave myself an F! What I had taught was true. I had not taught anything that I had come to believe was false. I had also not taught very much that spoke to the *Indian heart and mind* about God. I had presumed to know what they needed without really knowing them. I thank God for that lesson. Presumption comes in many forms. The cure however is always the same: humility.

Lectio Divina

> *When pride comes, then comes disgrace; but wisdom is with the humble. (Prov 11:2)*
>
> *Pride goes before destruction, and a haughty spirit before a fall. It is better to be of a lowly spirit among the poor than to divide the spoil with the proud. Those who are attentive to a matter will prosper, and happy are those who trust in the Lord. The wise of heart is called perceptive. (Prov 16:18-21a)*

Examen

Remember when Peter refused to confess Christ after he had promised never to abandon the Lord (Matt 26:33-35, 69-75). Reflect on a time in your life when your presumption caused you to fall or fail. Thank God that the Lord was there to ease the bitterness of your humiliation and to create in you a humble heart.

Prayer

> *Thank you gracious God for your beautiful gifts. You have created me in your own image. You have given me your Holy Spirit. Day by day, the likeness of Christ is being formed in my soul. You have invested me with talents and abilities. You have placed before me opportunities to shine. Thank you Lord, thank you. You are indeed like a parent who continually gives gifts to a child. With*

you, everyday is like Christmas. I ask now for the gift of perspective. Help me to remember that your image in me is marred by sin. Help me to remember that within me two spirits are at war. Remind me that the likeness of Christ in me is not yet fully formed. In spite of talents and abilities, let me not think more highly of myself than I ought. May I never forget that the light should shine on you and not me. I am still a child. Keep me from the sin of presumption. In the name of Jesus, I pray. Amen.

Day Three

The beauty and goodness and joy of created things are means for knowing and enjoying things divine.[3]

Selah

Perhaps because of the danger of worshiping the creation rather than the Creator, the Bible has little to say about finding God in the midst of nature. But the little it says is beautiful indeed!

In trying to help Job (and us) understand God, chapters 38–41 of Job speak of the majesty and unspeakable wisdom of God revealed through creation. It is an amazing list of animate and inanimate aspects of nature, all of which point to a knowledge of God that can be found in nature.

Like the psalmist, Paul affirmed that God's power and nature are revealed through what God has made. In light of this, we can understand Paul's reference to meditating on what is beautiful ("pleasing") as a reference to the beauties of creation.[4]

Lectio Divina

The heavens are telling the glory of God; and the firmament proclaims his handiwork. Day to day pours forth speech, and night to night declares knowledge. There is no speech, nor are there words; their voice is not heard. . . . In the heavens he has set a tent for the sun, which comes out like a bridegroom from his wedding canopy, and like a strong man runs its course with joy. Its rising is from the end of the heavens, and its circuit to the end of them; and nothing is hid from its heat. (Ps 19:1-4)

Bless the LORD, O my soul. O LORD my God, you are very great. You are clothed with honor and majesty, wrapped in light as with a garment. You stretch out the heavens like a tent, . . . you make the clouds your chariot, you ride on the wings of the wind. . . . You make springs gush forth in the valleys. . . . By the streams the

38

birds of the air have their habitation; they sing among the branches. . . . You cause the grass to grow for the cattle, and plants for people to use. . . . The high mountains are for the wild goats; the rocks are a refuge for the coneys. You have made the moon . . . [and] the sun. . . . O LORD, how manifold are your works! In wisdom you have made them all; the earth is full of your creatures. Yonder is the sea, great and wide. . . . May the glory of the LORD endure forever; may the LORD rejoice in his works. (Ps 104:1-3, 10, 12, 14, 18-19, 24-25, 31)

Examen

Today look at what God has made and marvel at the wisdom, creativity, and power that meet your eyes.

Prayer

Mighty Creator, maker of heaven and earth, I praise you. With the psalmist, I see your glory shining through the stars at night, glowing in the eyes of a graceful black cat, glistening in the morning dew. I smell your glory in the scent of roses and salty ocean. I hear your glory with the crashing of thunder and the chirping of songbirds. The taste of your glory is in wine and bread and blackberries. The texture of your glory is felt as I stroke a puppy or cradle a little baby. None of these things are you, O Lord. But in them I see reflected your beauty, your goodness, your truth. Thank you my Lord. Amen.

Day Four

The more souls immerse themselves in Him, the more they participate in His joyful Being.[5]

Selah

Joy is a mark of the Christian life. John 15:1-11 contains one of the more familiar nature analogies Jesus used in expressing the mysteries of the Christian life. He compared it to branches connected to a vine and tended by the vinegrower.

We often emphasize that God is love or God is holy. The Bible also teaches that God is joy. To know God is to know joy, a joy not destroyed by the trials of life.

Catherine knew suffering, pain, and sorrow. She saw people whom she loved suffer and die in the most painful ways. She experienced in her own body and mind the ravages of disease. She cried and wept in the pain of it all. Outwardly, her life may have looked like a portrait in various shades of pain; but inwardly, her life was colored with the bright hues of joy.

Lectio Divina

I am the true vine, and my Father is the vinegrower. He removes every branch in me that bears no fruit. Every branch that bears fruit he prunes to make it bear more fruit. You have already been cleansed by the word that I have spoken to you. Abide in me as I abide in you. Just as the branch cannot bear fruit by itself unless it abides in the vine, neither can you unless you abide in me. I am the vine, you are the branches. Those who abide in me and I in them bear much fruit because apart from me you can do nothing. Whoever does not abide in me is thrown away like a branch and withers; such branches are gathered, thrown into the fire, and burned. If you abide in me, and my words abide in you, ask for whatever you wish, and it will be done for you. My Father is glorified by this, that you bear much fruit and become my disciples.

40

As the Father has loved me, so I have loved you; abide in my love. If you keep my commandments, you will abide in my love, just as I have kept my Father's commandments and abide in his love. I have said these things to you so that my joy may be in you, and that your joy may be complete. (John 15:1-11)

Examen

Today think about the love of God, and rejoice. Think about Christ, and rejoice. Remember that the Spirit lives in you, and rejoice. Say the word "grace," and rejoice. Breath in the peace of God, and breath out the joy that fills your being.

Prayer

God of glory, God of grace, God of joy, I praise your name. I thank you for the gift of joy. I thank you for lips that can smile, for a voice that can break into laughter, for eyes that twinkle with gladness. I thank you that these gifts flow from a heart that is filled with your joy. May the joy I know overflow into the lives of those around me. For the sake of your name. Amen.

Day Five

You make all things bearable.[6]

Selah

Many Asian Christians would list 1 Corinthians 10:13 as their favorite scripture. Perhaps they love it so much because they have suffered so much. In Nepal and Malaysia, they have been imprisoned. In India, they have been disowned by their families. In Thailand, they have been ostracized by their former friends. Martyrs for the faith can be named in almost every country in Asia.

I confess to having little patience with those who cry over what passes as suffering for the faith in the Western world—may God make me more understanding. Nevertheless, the same grace that enables the Christians of Asia to endure physical and emotional abuse is available to help us who "endure" lesser strains.

I have found it helpful from time to time to reflect on the lives of early missionaries. It gives me greater strength when I read of the faithfulness of persons such as William Carey, Adoniram and Ann Judson, and Lottie Moon. In all likelihood, they suffered more than I ever will. Nevertheless, they persevered. They found the grace to bear up under the pains of imprisonment, the agony of dying children and spouses, the aching loneliness of separation from family.

Lectio Divina

> *No testing has overtaken you that is not common to everyone. God is faithful, and he will not let you be tested beyond your strength, but with the testing he will also provide the way out so that you may be able to endure it. (1 Cor 10:13)*

Examen

Our strength comes "through him who strengthens me" (Phil 4:12-13). It comes through Christ Jesus, the burden bearer. Memorize these words of Jesus: "Come to me, all you that are weary and carrying heavy burdens, and I will give you rest" (Matt 11:28). When you go to bed at night, say these words, and then sleep in faith. Perhaps you will awaken with renewed strength to face the day.

Prayer

Thank you Lord Jesus for these words of comfort. Thank you for the many evidences of your power and peace in the lives of Christians from all walks of life. I confess I worry too much. Bills, relationships, vocation, even the weather—I worry too much. I know it is a waste of time. Help me to worry less and to trust more. Today help me to believe that you are with me and that you really do want to carry my burdens, however heavy or insignificant they may be. Thank you Jesus. You are my Savior. You are my friend. Amen.

Day Six

If we are to become perfect, the change must be brought about in us and without us; that is, the change is to be the work not of man but of God. . . . [It is the work of] the pure and intense love of God alone.7

Selah

Jesus commands of us a perfection of love. It is not, however, primarily a feeling. It is the doing of good to everyone, even our enemies. Just as God blesses God's enemies with sunshine and rain, so should we be blessings to our enemies. We are to pray for them. We are to seek their well-being. The implication is that we will also do the same for our friends and casual acquaintances.

Reading the words of Jesus in Matthew 5 may cause two different reactions. Some persons will throw up their hands in futility, saying such love is impossible for humans. Others will say that Jesus did not mean exactly what he said, but he meant only that we should strive for such perfection. I think both responses are inappropriate.

Catherine understood that true perfection was a work of God. If fulfilling the command for perfection depended on human strength, we well might give up in despair. But despair is emotional blasphemy in the face of God's plan for our lives.

Paul wrote,

We know that all things work together for good for those who love God, who are called according to his purpose. For those whom he foreknew he also predestined to be conformed to the image of his Son. (Rom 8:28-29)

The destiny of every believer is to be conformed to the image of Jesus who was himself the perfect image of God in human form. We must never believe that our destiny awaits us only in heaven. Already we are being transformed. Already beams of love are shining through the good deeds of our lives.

MEDITATIONS

Lectio Divina

You have heard that it was said, "You shall love your neighbor and hate your enemy." But I say to you, Love your enemies and pray for those who persecute you, so that you may be children of your Father in heaven; for he makes his sun rise on the evil and on the good, and sends rain on the righteous and on the unrighteous. For if you love those who love you, what reward do you have? Do not even the tax collectors do the same? And if you greet only your brothers and sisters, what more are you doing than others? Do not even the Gentiles do the same? Be perfect, therefore, as your heavenly Father is perfect. (Matt 5:43-48)

Examen

Pray for perfection. Pray that today you will manifest the beautiful love of Christ for everyone you meet. That love may be shown as a friendly greeting, a smile, a warm handshake, a listening ear, a prayer, an act of kindness.

Prayer

Blessed God and Savior, you have called me to a life of perfection. You have called me to love my enemies. Such love is impossible for me. Some days, I can't even seem to love my friends. My heart is cold, and my will is weak. I don't want my life to be that way. I want to be like Jesus. I do want to love my friends, my enemies, and those anonymous people I pass on the street. Pour your love into my heart. Stengthen my will to move in kindness toward my neighbor—that person in need. I thank you Lord. I thank you that I am asking what you already desire to give. Today, let me be more like you. For the sake of your Name. Amen.

Day Seven

O love, who shall impede me from loving Thee?[8]

Selah

One day a Friar and Preacher, perhaps to test her or because of some mistaken notion, told her that he himself was better fitted for loving than she, because he having entered Religion and renounced all things both within and without, and she being married to the world as he was to Religion, he found himself more free to love God, and more acted upon by Him. And the Friar went on, and alleged many other reasons. But when he had spoken much and long, an ardent flame of pure love seized upon Catherine, and she sprang to her feet with such fervour as to appear beside herself, and she said: "If I thought that your habit had the power of gaining me one single additional spark of love, I should without fail take it from you by force, if I were not allowed to have it otherwise. That you should merit more than myself, is a matter that I concede and do not seek, I leave it in your hands; but that I cannot love Him as much as you, is a thing that you will never by any means be able to make me understand." [She returned home and cried out to God,] "O love, who shall impede me from loving Thee? though I were, not only in the world as I am, but in a camp of soldiers, I could not be impeded from loving thee."[9]

Lectio Divina

But God chose what is foolish in the world to shame the wise; God chose what is weak in the world to shame the strong; God chose what is low and despised in the world, things that are not, to reduce to nothing things that are, so that no one might boast in the presence of God. (1 Cor 1:27-29)

As many of you as were baptized into Christ have clothed yourselves with Christ. There is no longer Jew or Greek, there is no longer slave or free, there is no longer male and female; for all of you are one in Christ Jesus. (Gal 3:27-28)

46

MEDITATIONS

Examen

Think about how much God loves you and all persons. On a scale of 1 to 10, how strong is God's love? That is the easy answer. On a scale of 1 to 10, how strong is your love for God? How does it compare to Catherine's love? Does God love her more than you? As you reflect on the answers to these questions, allow your thoughts to become prayer.

Prayer

Thank you Lord Jesus for revealing to the world the impartiality of our God. You ate with the rich and the poor. You taught the scholar and the uneducated. You touched Jew and Gentile. You allowed men and women to follow you. You prayed for the children and the elderly. In your life we see the beautiful reflection of the love of God for all persons. Truly God shows no partiality. Now I thank you Lord for the life of your servant, Catherine of Genoa. I thank you that by your grace she was able to show love to the needy, ministering to their pain and sorrow. I thank you that by your grace she was ablaze with an undying love for you. May such grace be mine. In Jesus' name. Amen.

Notes

[1]Catherine of Genoa, quoted in Benedict J. Groeschel, "The Spiritual Dialogue," *Catherine of Genoa: Purgation and Purgatory, The Spiritual Dialogue*, Serge Hughes, trans. (New York: Paulist Press, 1979) 78.

[2]Friedrich von Hugel, *The Mystical Element of Religion as Studied in Saint Catherine of Genoa and Her Friends*, 2 vols. (London: J. M. Dent & Sons Ltd., 1908) 1:271.

[3]Catherine, *The Spiritual Dialogue*, 102.

[4]Ibid., 86.

[5]LaMon Brown, "Pauline Mysticism in His Epistle to the Philippians" *Theological Educator*, Fall 1980, 55-60.

[6]Catherine, *The Spiritual Dialogue*, 145.

[7]Ibid., 81.

[8]Von Hugel, 1:141.

[9]Ibid., 140-141.

WILLIAM LAW

❧ 1 ❧

DISCIPLINED
NONCONFORMIST

Wherever thou goest, whatever thou dost, at Home, or Abroad, in the Field, or at Church, do all in a Desire of Union with Christ, in Imitation of his Tempers and Inclinations, and look upon all as Nothing, but that which exercises, and increases the Spirit and Life of Christ in thy Soul. From Morning to Night keep Jesus in thy Heart, long for Nothing, desire Nothing, hope for Nothing, but to have all that is within Thee changed into the spirit and Temper of the Holy Jesus. Let this be thy Christianity, thy Church, and thy Religion.[1]

Selah

William Law appeared destined for great things in the Church of England. He was born in 1686 into a locally respected and genteel family.[2] He received his bachelor's and master's degrees from Emmanuel College of Cambridge. In 1711, he was ordained as a deacon and elected to a fellowship at his college. His future looked bright indeed.

In 1714, however, he and a minority of other ordained persons refused to swear allegiance to King George I of the House of Hanover. Law and others believed that the kingship of England had been given to the Stuarts by God as divine right. Because of his refusal to swear the oath, Law lost his fellowship and all possibility of future church appointments. He then had to earn a living as a tutor, private chaplain, and writer.

In 1723, he became the tutor in the household of Edward Gibbons, father of the famous historian. He maintained this position for ten years until the younger Edward finished his college years. During this period William Law wrote the book that has cemented his name in the annals of Christian devotional writers: *A Serious Call to a Devout and Holy Life.*

Law himself was serious about religion. As a young adult going off to college, he compiled a list of eighteen rules. Among them were the following:

> To fix it deep in my mind, that I have but one business upon my hands, to seek for eternal happiness, by doing the will of God. . . . To think nothing great or desirable, because the world thinks it so; but to form all my judgements of things from the infallible Word of God, and direct my life according to it. . . . To avoid all excess in eating and drinking. . . . To be always fearful of letting my time slip away without some fruit. . . . To call to mind the presence of God, whenever I find myself under temptation to sin, and to have immediate recourse to prayer. . . . To think humbly of myself and with great charity of all others. . . . To think often of the life of Christ, and propose it as a pattern for myself. . . . To pray, privately, thrice a day, besides my morning and evening prayers. . . . To spend some time giving an account of the day, previous to evening prayer: How have I spent this day? What sin have I committed? What temptations have I withstood? Have I performed all my duties?[3]

Around 1740, Law made his final move. Miss Hester Gibbons and Mrs. Sarah Hutchenson, a wealthy pious widow, invited him to move into their recently purchased house in his hometown of King's Cliffe. He lived there as their spiritual director and chaplain for some twenty-one years until his death due to kidney disease in 1761. While serving in this capacity, he also wrote a number of other works, including *The Spirit of Prayer,* which contains the opening quotation of this chapter.

The household divided its time between religious exercises and works of charity. Both Gibbons and Hutchenson had inheritance incomes, and Law received money from his books as well as from other benefactors who admired his work. They used 10 percent of their income to care for their own needs. The remainder went to various charitable works.

Law founded a school for poor girls. They were taught to read, sew, and knit, and were instructed in the Anglican catechism and taken to church services regularly. Mrs. Hutchensen started a second girls school and an almshouse for the poor.

In addition to the institutional works, they also distributed clothing, food, and money to the poor. The surrounding community disapproved of these works, accusing Law and the others of attracting the idle and worthless to King's Cliffe. Yet, the works of charity continued.

A typical day at King's Cliffe started at 5 A.M. Law arose to spend some time in private devotions. Afterwards he had a light breakfast and then began a period of study. Family devotion time was set for 9 A.M. Between the end of these devotions and a noon lunch, Law returned to his books and study. After lunch, he gathered with the two ladies of the house for a period of devotional exercises. More individual study followed until teatime. After tea, devotions resumed with the servants often taking turns reading a chapter from the Bible.

In spite of this tightly structured schedule, Law never forgot about the poor. Every morning he personally distributed milk to them. He also gave out money, clothes, or food as needed. He made sure the food was tasty and the clothing clean and in good repair.[4]

It is not clear if Law carried his nonjuror beliefs with him to the grave. Although he did not always get along with the local priest, he was a faithful member of the parish church, regularly attending all services. In addition to his personal devotional exercises, he obviously felt that participation in a local church was an important part of the Christian life.

Reading the code of the young Law and his later *A Serious Call*, one could believe he was a rather dour person. His natural personality was introverted. Some of his contemporaries spoke of his unsmiling demeanor. Nevertheless, those closest to him affirmed that he was often filled with the joy of the Lord. In fact, as he lay dying, he sang a hymn.[5]

Some of his later interpreters believe the older Law and the younger Law had radically different views of the Christian life. The younger Law wrote, among other works, *A Treatise on Christian Perfection* and *A Serious Call to a Devout and Holy Life*. His later works include *The Spirit of Prayer, The Way of Divine Knowledge,* and *The Spirit of Love.*

Law's later works were obviously influenced by his study of the writings of the Protestant mystic, Jacob Boehme, whom Law apparently began reading some time between 1735 and 1740. Whereas the younger Law stressed rules and methods, the older Law seemed at times to disdain such aids to devotion and call only for a total surrender of self to God. Austin Warren suggested that the later Law forgot the many years he had spent in preparing for this higher life.[6]

The distinction between the early and the later Law can be too sharply stated, however. Another commentator, Erwin Rudolph, wrote that when Law became a follower of Boehme's writings, he never recanted anything he had written earlier. Neither did his reverence for Scripture decline.[7]

In the final analysis, the debate between Law scholars should not discourage us in looking to him for guidance in the area of spiritual disciplines. My own feeling is that Law's continued practice of devotional exercises and attendance at worship services indicate he did not truly "forget" the path he had trod. His later works do not stress rules and methods because he had already affirmed their need and chose to address other matters and concerns.

Lectio Divina

> *I am grateful to God—whom I worship with a clear conscience, as my ancestors did—when I remember you constantly in my prayers night and day. Recalling your tears, I long to see you so that I may be filled with joy. I am reminded of your sincere faith, a faith that lived first in your grandmother Lois and your mother Eunice and now, I am sure, lives in you. For this reason I remind you to rekindle the gift of God that is within you through the laying on of my hands; for God did not give us a spirit of cowardice, but rather a spirit of power and of love and of self-discipline. (2 Tim 1:3-7)*

Examen

Power, love, and self-discipline were evident in the life of William Law. The power of his writing to influence the lives of people is well known. His love of others, which manifested itself in service to the needy, is noteworthy. The rigorous discipline of his spiritual life is daunting. However, pray not that God will turn you into a William Law, but that God will bless you with power, love, and discipline that are appropriate for who you are and where you are. Take a moment before you pray to note areas of your life where those three marks are already evident in some degree. Then begin by thanking God for those beginnings.

Prayer

O God of Paul and Timothy and William Law, I thank you that by your grace their lives manifested power, love, and discipline. I thank you that even in my life I have found evidences of godly power, love, and discipline. Specifically I thank you for _____ [insert the marks of your life]. May these evidences of your grace grow until I am like the Perfect One. I pray in his name, the name of Jesus. Amen.

Notes

[1] *The Spirit of Prayer; or, the Soul Rising out of the Vanity of Time into the Riches of Eternity* (London: M. Richardson, 1749) 24, in *The Works of the Reverend William Law*, vol. 7 (New York: Hildesheim, 1974).

[2] Unless otherwise noted, the standard biographical notes are from Austin Warren, "William Law: Ascetic and Mystic," introduction to *William Law: A Serious Call to a Devout and Holy Life [and] The Spirit of Love*, edited by Paul G. Stanwood (New York: Paulist Press, 1978).

[3] A. Keith Walker, *William Law: His Life and Thought* (London: S.P.C.K., 1973) 3-4.

[4] Erwin Paul Rudolph, *William Law* (Boston: Twayne Publishers, 1980) 15.

[5] Rudolph, 16.

[6] Warren, 31.

[7] Rudolph, 89.

❧2❧

PRAYER

"Prayer is the nearest approach to God and the highest enjoyment of Him that we are capable of in this life."[1]

Selah

William Law recommended certain basics for all types of prayer. We are to kneel, close our eyes, and in silence place ourselves in the presence of God.[2] In many books on prayer this is called recollection. It is the calling of ourselves away from the distractions of the world; it is the collecting of ourselves before God.

Law also suggested beginning each prayer with a psalm. Chanting or singing the psalm is better than merely reading it, since singing stirs our hearts more than reading.[3] He suggested specifically Psalms 34, 96, 103, 111, 145, 146, and 147, but stressed that we should be free to make our own selection.[4]

Law encourages us to think of the attributes and activities of God in the beginning of our prayers, affirming God's power and greatness. Collecting appropriate material can help us in this and in the other parts of our prayer life. According to Law,

> When at any time, either in reading the Scripture or any book of piety, you meet with a passage that more than ordinarily affects your mind and seems as it were to give your heart a new motion toward God, you should try to turn it into the form of a petition, and then give it a place in your prayers.[5]

He also encourages us to collect the best forms of devotion and the finest passages of Scripture, for these can help us when we pray.[6]

Law believed that these collected and written forms of prayer could benefit anyone, but he recognized that others might have a better way of prayer for themselves:

If anyone can find a better way of raising his heart to God in private than by prepared forms of prayer, I have nothing to object against it.[7]

He advocated the use of imagination.[8] Especially when using the Psalms, he suggested imagining ourselves singing with Jesus or with David. Law also mentioned picturing the hosts of heaven praising God as in Revelation 7:9-12. The specifics of his program included six times of prayer each day, with appropriate topics for each prayer period.

Law wrote, "I take it for granted that every Christian that is in health is up early in the morning."[9] More will be said later about how Law's system can be adapted for those who do not have a lifestyle conducive to a literal following of his suggestions. And the fact of the matter is he did not so take it for granted, for he spent the next several pages of *A Serious Call* berating lazy, self-indulgent Christians.

To encourage his readers, Law stressed certain advantages to early prayer: It involves self-denial, it is a way to renounce indulgence, it is a means to redeem one's time, and it helps prepare a person's spirit to receive the Spirit of God.[10] He described this period of prayer thus:

Your first devotions should be a praise and thanksgiving to God, as for a new creation; and . . . you should offer and devote your body and soul, all that you are and all that you have, to His service and glory. Receive every day as a resurrection from death, as a new enjoyment of life; meet every rising sun with such sentiments of God's goodness as if you had seen it and all things new created upon your account; and under the sense of so great a blessing, let your joyful heart praise and magnify so good and glorious a Creator.[11]

Our first prayers, then, are to include an offering of ourselves anew to God with a spirit of praise and thanksgiving.

The rest of Law's system may be summarized. At 9 A.M., humility is the prayer topic. At noon, it is universal love that manifests itself in intercession for others. At 3 P.M., resignation to God's will is the suggested thought for prayer. At 6 P.M., one should pray prayers of confession. At bedtime, death is the most appropriate topic.

Law commended the topic of humility because he felt it is crucial for the Christian life.

> Humility is the life and soul of piety, the foundation and support of every virtue and good work, the best guard and security of all holy affections. . . . We may as well think to see without eyes or live without breath as to live in the spirit of religion without the spirit of humility.[12]

He was so convinced of the need for humility that he spent far more time on it than any other prayer topic. In fact, he devoted four full chapters of his book to it. In one chapter he specifies that we can cultivate a proper sense of humility by recognizing our limitations and sin, by comparing glorious heaven to our fallen world, and by contemplating the picture of our crucified Lord.[13]

God is love, and Christ has given us the perfect example of that love in practice. Such were reasons enough for Law to choose universal love for the noon topic.[14] Intercession or praying for others is a natural response of such love.

The benefits of intercession include an increase in friendship among Christians and other relations, a greater measure of fulfillment concerning each person's duties, a lessening of wrong feelings such as spite and envy, and a clearer picture of the condition of the praying person's heart.[15]

For many years, this sentence from Law has affected my own appreciation of intercessory prayer: "There is nothing that makes us love a man so much as praying for him."[16] I have found it increasingly difficult to hold ill feelings toward people for whom I am praying. May God help me to pray more often for them!

Resignation and conformity to God's will is the virtue recommended for consideration at 3 P.M. Law believed that God has a general providence for the world and a particular providence for each individual. If we are to practice the virtue of resignation, we must thankfully accept whatever happens to us as allowed by God for God's own good and perfect purposes. Law was quick to say that just because God permits something to happen, this does not mean the occurrence is therefore just or right; otherwise, nothing would be unjust or unrighteous.[17]

I confess that I find this position unsatisfying. I think it is wrong to accept with thanksgiving all things that happen to us. Even if God does allow them, some are not pleasing to God. For example, the Lord said, "I have no pleasure in the death of anyone" (Ezek 18:32a).

Rather than offer thankful acceptance to God for every happening in my day, I would prefer one or two other topics that are related to the issue: a prayer renewing my morning commitment to God or a prayer asking for patience. The following is an example of the kind of prayer I might pray. It is modeled on a prayer by Georgia Harkness.[18]

> O God my Father, it is good to know that whatever happens to me that you are my rock and my salvation. Deliver me from evil. Help me to believe that you will never leave me alone or that nothing can defeat you—for this is true deliverance. It comforts me to realize that you know my life, my weaknesses, my mortality. You never allow my burdens to become too great. Give me patience in the midst of trouble. Grant me to have understanding, humility, self-restraint, and power. Father, into your hands I again commit myself. Do with me as you will, through Jesus your Son and my Lord. Amen.

William Law called for an evening prayer of specific confession and repentance, which can only be performed after a true self-examination.[19] In an age still aglow with "I'm OK; you're OK," it is good to remind ourselves that we are sinners. Our sin may lie in what we have done, in what we have not done, in what we have harbored in our hearts, or in what we have allowed to evaporate from our hearts. A careful examination of each of these areas may prove enlightening. From that truth can come true confession and repentance.

Bedtime is the last opportunity for prayer before one goes to sleep. William Law felt that death could easily be pictured in the likeness of sleep and darkness. Such a time of prayer would remind us of our utter dependence on God for life. Compared to the other topics, Law devoted only a few lines to this time of prayer. Yet I was reminded of my own childhood prayer: "As I lay me down to sleep, I pray the Lord my soul to keep. And if I die before I wake, I pray the Lord my soul to take." I am sure some folks cringe to think of a little child praying about death; but, at least in my case, it did no harm. In fact, I suspect it reinforced in me a confidence in God.

Law's system certainly worked for him. It has worked for many others as well. However, both Law and those others were people who had "free" time to devote significant portions of the day to prayer. What about people who work eight hours a day in a factory or an institution that requires constant attention to the work at hand? How can they devote fifteen to thirty minutes or more to prayer at 9 A.M., noon, and 3 P.M.? My suggestion is to use what we can and adapt the rest. The following is a possible prayer schedule most folks can keep.

Begin the day with prayers of praise and surrender. Read a praise psalm, and let it lead you in prayer. Call to mind Jesus' experience in the garden of Gethsemane. Make "not my will, but your will be done" a regular part of your heart's prayer. Of course, you can find other instances of praise and surrender that may help you in this morning time. As Law suggested, it would be a good idea to collect prayers of this type.[21]

At your midday meal, include at least one specific note of intercession in your prayer of thanksgiving. Even before you arise from your morning devotions, ask God to give you the name of a person for whom you may pray later in the day.

In the evening, make some time for prayers of confession and thanksgiving. You can incorporate the material on the prayer of examen mentioned in chapter 1.

At bedtime, place yourself in God's hands. Jesus talked about the need to become as children. Perhaps that childhood prayer of mine would still be appropriate to close the day.

What about the rest of the day? I have practiced two slightly different techniques. Sometimes, attempting to follow Law's scheme in spirit, if not in the letter, I have set my watch for 9 A.M. and 3 P.M. If it was convenient, I would pause for just a moment at those times. At 9:00, I would pray for humility. At 3:00, I would pray for patience and strength to follow God's will.

Another technique I have used is setting my watch to beep every hour. At the beep, I would voice maybe just a sentence such as "Lord Jesus Christ, have mercy on me" or "My Lord, I love you." If you don't have a programmable watch, discipline yourself to speak a word to God when you hear a clock chiming, a bell ringing, or a horn blowing. Prayer is turning our attention to God. We should use every means to help us not forget about God's presence in the midst of our hectic days and nights.

Before we decide that Law's system, even in a modified version, is too much for a person of our fast paced world, let us read his response to those who complained—even in his day—that his proposed hours of prayer came too quickly one upon the other:

> This method of devotion is not pressed upon any sort of people as absolutely necessary, but recommended to all people as the best, happiest, and most perfect way of life. . . . Most men of business and figure engage too far in worldly matters, much farther than the reasons of human life or the necessities of the world require. Merchants and tradesmen, for instance, are generally ten times further engaged in business than they need, which so far from being a reasonable excuse for their want of time for devotion that it is their crime and must be censured as a blamable instance of covetousness and ambitions. . . .

> If a merchant, having forbore from too great a business that he might quietly attend to the service of God, should therefore die worth twenty instead of fifty thousand pounds, could anyone say that he had mistaken his calling, or gone a loser out of the world? . . .

> If a tradesman, by aspiring after Christian perfection and retiring himself often from his business, instead of leaving his children fortunes to spend in luxury and idleness, leave them to live by their own honest labor, could it be said that he had made a wrong use of the world? . . .

> Since . . . devotion is . . . the best and most desirable practice of men, as men, and in every state of life, they that desire to be excused

from it because they are men of figure and estates and business are no wiser than those that should desire to be excused from health and happiness because they were men of figure and estates. . . .

You would think it very absurd for a man not to value his own health because he was not a physician, or the preservation of his limbs because he was not a bone-setter. Yet it is more absurd for you . . . to neglect the improvement of your soul in piety because you are not an Apostle or a bishop, [or as we might say, a full-time Christian worker].[22]

Lectio Divina

He [Jesus] was praying in a certain place, and after he had finished, one of his disciples said to him, "Lord, teach us to pray, as John taught his disciples." He said to them, "When you pray, say: 'Father, hallowed be your name. Your kingdom come. Give us each day our daily bread. And forgive us our sins, for we ourselves forgive everyone indebted to us. And do not bring us to the time of trial.'. . . 'If you, then who are evil, know how to give good gifts to your children, how much more will the heavenly Father give the Holy Spirit to those who ask him!'" (Luke 11:1-4, 13)

Likewise the Spirit helps us in our weakness; for we do not know how to pray as we ought, but that very Spirit intercedes with sighs too deep for words. And God, who searches the heart, knows what is the mind of the Spirit, because the Spirit intercedes for the saints according to the will of God. (Rom 8:26-27)

Examen

Take some time today to determine how and when you want to pray during the next month. Write out your commitment, but remember that occasional failures along the way are no reason to give up. If I forget to eat lunch one day, I am not going to give it up forever!

63

Prayer

O God who hears our prayers, I come to you. Whenever I pray, guide my thoughts by the spirit of Jesus. Help me to pray with his intensity. Help me to pray with his regularity. Help me to pray with his clarity. In the name of Jesus, the man of prayer. Amen.

Notes

[1] William Law, *A Serious Call to a Devout and Holy Life*, in *William Law: A Serious Call to a Devout and Holy Life [and] The Spirit of Love*, edited by Paul G. Stanwood (New York: Paulist Press, 1978) 189-90.

[2] Ibid., 198.

[3] Ibid., 209-10.

[4] Ibid., 224.

[5] Ibid., 200.

[6] Ibid., 203.

[7] Ibid., 196-97.

[8] Ibid., 222-23. Two sources that help to describe the appropriate use of imagination in prayer are Morton T. Kelsey, *The Other Side of Silence: A Guide to Christian Meditation* (New York: Paulist Press, 1976) and Richard Foster, *Celebration of Discipline: The Path to Spiritual Growth* (New York: HarperCollins, 1978, rev. ed. 1988).

[9] Ibid., 189.

[10] Ibid., 195-96.

[11] Ibid., 200-201.

[12] Ibid., 228.

[13] Ibid., 229-32.

[14] Ibid., 288-90.

[15] Ibid., 315.

[16] Ibid., 302.

[17] Ibid., 318-20.

[18] Georgia Harkness, *The Glory of God: Poems and Prayers for Devotional Use* (New York: Abingdon-Cokesbury Press, 1943) 77.

[19] Law, *Serious Call*, 328-29.

[20] Ibid., 340.

[21] Two sources that contain prayers of praise and surrender are E. Glenn Hinson, *The Reaffirmation of Prayer* (Nashville: Broadman Press, 1979) 141-49; and John Baille, *A Diary of Private Prayer* (New York: Charles Scribner's Sons, 1949).

[22] Law, *Serious Call*, 280-83.

❧3❧
STUDY

Why then must the Bible lie alone in your study? Is not the spirit of the saints, the piety of the holy followers of Jesus Christ, as good and necessary a means as entering into the spirit and taste of the gospel as the reading of the ancients is of entering into the spirit of antiquity?

Is the spirit of poetry only to be got by much reading of poets and orators? And is not the spirit of devotion to be got in the same way, by frequent reading of the holy thoughts and pious strains of devout men?[1]

Selah

Study was important to William Law. In reading the code he drew up to guide himself during his years as a student, it is obvious he desired to use his time wisely in studies that would promote his growth in the image of Christ. As a lifelong discipline, he withdrew daily to his study for several extended periods of reading and reflection.

He loved the Bible, especially the New Testament. His writings are full of references to Scripture. From first to last he seeks to expound the truth of God's Word. Clearly he spent long hours reading and reflecting on the Bible, but he also found the study of other writings of great benefit.

In his first substantial work Law wrote,

Reading, when it is an Exercise of the Mind upon wise and pious Subjects, is, next to *Prayer,* the best Improvement of our Hearts. It enlightens our Minds, collects our Thoughts, calms and allays our Passions, and begets in us so many Benefits, that does so much Good to our Minds, that it ought never to be employed amiss: It enters so far into our Souls, that it cannot have a little Effect upon us. We commonly say, that a Man is known by his *Companions;* but it is certain, that a Man is much more known by the Books that he converses with. These *Closet- companions* with whom we choose to be alone and in private, are never-failing Proofs of the State and Disposition of our Hearts.[2]

Almost fifteen years later, in a polemical writing, Law specified some of the writers he had studied in those long hours spent in his library:

> Of those Mystical Divines, I thank God, I have been a diligent Reader, through all Ages of the Church, from the Apostolical *Dionysius the Areopagite,* down to the great *Fenelon* Archbishop of *Cambray,* the illuminated *Guyon,* and M. *Bertot.* Had the Doctor read St. *Cassian,* a Recorder of the Lives, Spirit and Doctrine of the Holy Fathers of the *Deserts,* as often as he had read the *Story of Aeneas* and *Dido,* he had been less astonished at many Things in my Writings: But I apprehend the Doctor to be as great a Stranger to the Writers of this kind, with which every Age of the Church has been blessed, and to know no more of the Divine *Ruysbroeck, Tauler, Suso, Harphius, John of the Cross,* etc., than he does of *Jacob Boehme.* For had he known any Thing of them, he had known that I am as chargeable with the Sentiments of all of them, as with those of *J. Boehme.* For though I never wrote upon any subject till I could call it *my own,* till I was so fully possessed of the Truth of it, that I could sufficiently prove it in my *own Way,* without borrowed Arguments; yet Doctrines of Religion I have none, but what the Scriptures and the *first-rate* Saints of the Church are my Vouchers for.[3]

Sections of the present work on William Law and Catherine of Genoa are called *lectio divina.* This phrase, which can be translated as "holy reading," is a near synonym to what I mean by the discipline of study. Holy reading is not necessarily reading a great quantity of books. It is reading a few books well. It is reading to hear God address our lives. Holy Scripture holds the privileged place, but other books may be profitably read as well. In this reading we learn about God and about ourselves.

The best explanation of this discipline I have found is in a fine book by Aelred Squire. The following material on holy reading is largely distilled from his chapter devoted to that topic.[4] Squire found the following advice from William of St. Thierry:

> Further, you should spend certain periods of time in specific sorts of reading. For if you read now here, now there, the various things that chance and circumstance send, this does not consolidate you, but makes your spirit unstable. For it is easy to take such reading in and easier still to forget it. You ought rather to delay with certain minds and grow used to them. For the Scriptures need to be read in the same spirit in which they were written, and only in that spirit are they to be understood. You will never reach an understanding of Paul until, by close attention to reading him and the application of continual reflection, you imbibe his spirit. You will never arrive at understanding David until by the actual experience you realize what the Psalms are about. And so it is with the rest. In every piece of Scripture, real attention is as different from mere reading as friendship is from entertainment, or the love of a friend from a casual greeting.[5]

I remember the first time I read those words. I was sitting in my office at the Thailand Baptist Seminary in Bangkok. I was there, in part, to teach the Bible. When I finished reading that passage, I had to put the book down for a few minutes because my eyes were filled with tears. How trivial and perfunctory had been much of my reading of God's Word! At best, I had read to teach and preach rather than to hear. I had read to get rather than to receive.

William of St. Thierry also believed that

> if he who reads genuinely seeks God in his reading, anything he reads will promote his good, and his mind will grasp, and submit the meaning of his reading to the service of Christ.[6]

While this idea could be misused, the point may be understood as follows. If we have immersed ourselves in the truths of Scripture, and if we are truly seeking God, reading the works of others can be a great benefit to our spiritual growth. I will have more to say later about specific readings that have helped me, but for now let us note two other emphases from Squire's presentation.

Holy reading, whether Scripture or some other appropriate writing, is described by a selection from Jean-Pierre de Caussade who had sent a specific book for holy reading to a friend.

> If you are to get from it all the good I anticipate, you must not throw yourself greedily upon it or let yourself be drawn on by curiosity as to what comes next. Fix your attention upon what you are reading without thinking about what follows. I recommend you primarily to enter into the helpful and sure truths you will find in this book, by cultivating a taste for them rather than speculating about them. Pause briefly, from time to time, to let these pleasant truths sink deeper into your soul, and allow the Holy Spirit time to work. During these peaceful pauses and quiet waiting, he will engrave these heavenly truths upon your heart. Do it all without stifling your interests or making any violent efforts to avoid reflections. Simply let the truths sink into your heart rather than into your mind.[7]

Holy reading does not end when we put the book down. In order for what we have read to become a permanent part of our lives, we must take it back with us into life. Allow what you have read to impact the way you live and act.

What books would I recommend? Reading is often a very personal thing related to one's own circumstances. For instance, on one occasion when asked what books other than the Bible had most influenced me, I answered *The Great Divorce* by C. S. Lewis and *The Last Temptation of Christ* by Kazanzakis. Lewis's book helped me to overcome doubts about the reality of hell. The controversial book by Kazanzakis, in spite of its obvious weaknesses, enabled me to appreciate the humanity of Christ in a way I never had before.

Although these works were helpful to me, I certainly would not recommend them to everyone. The same could be said of two biographical works that have moved me: Janet Lynch-Watson's *The Saffron Robe*, a biography of the great Indian Christian Sadhu Sundar Singh; and C. G. Jung's enigmatic *Memories, Dreams, and Reflections*.

There are, however, only two books not related to a teaching or preaching assignment that I have read more than once. I recommend the anonymous work entitled *Theologia Germanica* (sometimes titled *German Theology*) and *The Practice of the Presence of God* by Brother Lawrence (or Nicholas Herman). In addition to these two, I would add the sermons of John Tauler and the writings of Evelyn Underhill. I have found both of these persons to be reliable guides in matters of spirituality.

Although the bulk of my discussion on the topic of study has related to the reading of books, in closing this section, it is appropriate to affirm other forms of study.

Study may relate to hearing rather than reading. This is good news for the millions of illiterate people in the world. It is also good news for millions more whose reading skills are too weak to tackle anything beyond the simplest sentences and vocabulary. This does not mean that only these two classes should take advantage of study through the sense of hearing. All of us could benefit from it.

The spoken work, either live or on tape, can be an effective medium to help us study. As in holy reading, we will need repetition, concentration, and reflection. For readers, I would mention that sometimes I have found reading aloud helps me to slow down and concentrate.

A form of study rarely if ever mentioned is the use of music. Earlier we noted that Law recommended chanting or singing the psalms because our hearts would more likely be moved. Whether we sing songs or listen to songs being sung, it can be an exercise in study. Repetition, concentration, and reflection with the desire to hear the voice of God makes it so.

Finally, we can also study the events of our lives. The Spirit of God is at work in our world. Let us listen for the Spirit's voice in the experiences of our lives and the lives of those around us.

In his book on spiritual disciplines, Dallas Willard sums up much of what this chapter is about.

> In study we also strive to see the Word of God at work in the lives of others, in the church, in history, and in nature. We not only read and hear and inquire, but we *meditate* on what comes before us; that is, we withdraw into silence where we prayerfully and steadily focus upon it. In this way its meaning for us can emerge and form us as

71

God works in the depths of our heart, mind, and soul. We devote long periods of time to this. Our prayer as we study meditatively is always that God would meet with us and speak specifically to us, for ultimately the Word of God is God speaking.[8]

Lectio Divina

Besides being wise, the Teacher also taught the people knowledge, weighing and studying and arranging many proverbs. The Teacher sought to find pleasing words, and he wrote words of truth plainly. The sayings of the wise are like goads, and like nails firmly fixed are the collected sayings that are given by one shepherd. (Eccl 12:9-11)

Examen

Ask God to help you choose a book of the Bible or a book by a spiritual master to study. Read a portion of it each day. The first time read the portion aloud for concentration. Read it a second time silently for repetition. Reflect on the passage as you pray and/or write in your journal.

Prayer

O you who were and are and are to come, I thank you that this Christian way on which I walk is no untried or uncharted road. It is a road beaten hard by the footsteps of saints, apostles, prophets, and martyrs. I thank you for the finger posts and danger signals with which it is marked at every turning and that may be known to me through the study of the Bible, and of all history, and of all the great literature of the world. Forbid it, Holy Lord, that I should fail to profit by these great memories of the ages gone by, or to enter into the glorious inheritance you have prepared for me. I pray through Jesus Christ our Lord. Amen.[9]

Notes

[1]William Law, *A Serious Call to a Devout and Holy Life*, in *William Law: A Serious Call to a Devout and Holy Life [and] The Spirit of Love*, edited by Paul G. Stanwood (New York: Paulist Press, 1978) 206.

[2]William Law, *A Practical Treatise upon Christian Perfection* (London: William and John Innys, 1726) 165, in *The Works of the Reverend William Law*, vol. 3 (New York: Hildesheim, 1974).

[3]William Law, *Some Animadversions upon Dr. Trapp's Late Reply* (London: W. Innys and J. Richardson, 1740) 157, in *The Works of the Reverend William Law*, vol. 6 (New York: Hildesheim, 1974). *Some Animadversions* was attached to a longer piece entitled (in part) *An Appeal to All That Doubt or Disbelieve the Truths of the Gospel*. In the passage quoted, I have changed the spelling of some of the names to correspond to the more accepted modern spelling.

[4]Aelred Squire, *Asking the Fathers: The Art of Meditation and Prayer* (New York: Paulist Press, 1973) 117-27.

[5]Ibid., 125.

[6]Ibid., 124.

[7]Ibid., 125

[8]Dallas Willard, *The Spirit of the Disciplines: Understanding How God Changes Lives* (New York: HarperCollins, 1988) 177.

[9]Adapted with slight modernization from John Baille, *A Diary of Private Prayer* (New York: Scribner's, 1945) 25.

4

SIMPLICITY

The two things which of all others most want to be under strict rule and which are the greatest blessings both to ourselves and to others when they are rightly used are our time and our money.[1]

Selah

In his *Serious Call*, William Law devoted four full chapters and significant parts of others to the discipline of simplicity. He believed strongly that as Christians we are compelled to the wise use of our material resources. He gave a number of reasons for using our resources wisely and religiously. Two seem to speak with great power.

First, we should use all of our financial resources or estate properly.

> It is capable of being used to the most excellent purposes and is so great a means of doing good. If we waste it, we don't waste a trifle that signifies little, but we waste that which might be made as eyes to the blind, as a husband to the widow, as a father to the orphan. We waste that which not only enables us to minister worldly comforts to those that are in distress, but that which might purchase for ourselves everlasting treasures in Heaven. So that if we part with our money in foolish ways, we part with a great power of comforting our fellow creatures and of making ourselves forever blessed.[2]

Second, to use our resources wrongly is to hurt ourselves.

> For so much as is spent in the vanity of dress may be reckoned so much laid out to fix vanity in our minds. So much as is laid out for idleness and indulgence may be reckoned so much given to render our hearts dull and sensual. So much as is spent in state and equipage may be reckoned so much spent to dazzle your own eyes, and render you the idol of your own imagination. And so in everything, when you go from reasonable wants, you only support some unreasonable temper, some turn of mind, which every good Christian is called upon to renounce.[3]

Law pointed to certain biblical texts to support his call to the right use of money, and then illustrated the wrong use of one's own finances. He named the character Flavia. Lest we think he found such living more visible in the lives of women, he used a female character, Miranda, to illustrate frugality.

Miranda, the good example, refused to "indulge herself in needless vain expenses." Instead, as a duty to God, she lived so simply that the only difference between her and the poor was that she had "the blessedness of giving." Her rule concerning clothing was to be always clean and "in the cheapest things."[4] Miranda blessed the lives of many people by the wise use of her resources. William Law encouraged women to follow the example of Miranda and called on all persons of every walk of life to live right before God and in the world.

> Bended knees, whilst you are clothed with pride; heavenly petitions, whilst you are hoarding up treasures upon earth; holy devotions, whilst you live in the follies of the world; prayers of meekness and charity, whilst your heart is the seat of spite and resentment; hours of prayer, whilst you give up days and years to idle diversions, impertinent visits, and foolish pleasures are as absurd, unacceptable service to God as forms of thanksgiving from a person who lives in repinings and discontent.[5]

Law practiced what he wrote. He lived frugally and gave away much to the needy. The following are a few examples from his life at King's Cliffe.[6]

The combined incomes of the three living there were not inconsiderable. However, they spent so little on themselves and refused to accumulate a large sum that, when Law and the two ladies died, the inhabitants of the village spoke of their boundless acts of charity.

They built schools for children and houses for widows. They gave money regularly to widows and other poor persons and distributed food and clothing. One interesting sidelight to the clothing giveaway illustrates Law's commitment to simplicity. Among the clothes given to the poor were coarse linen shirts. In order that Law might not be tempted to give away what he himself might refuse, he customarily wore the shirts and then washed them before giving them away.

He also ate moderately and apparently from a wooden platter. It is surmised that he used wooden platters rather than plates in order to assist a local business.

His study was a simple four-foot square area separated from his bedroom by a wainscoting. It contained a chair, a desk, a Bible, and a few books.

Law's study of the New Testament convinced him of the Christian duty to wisely use our resources for the good of others. In *A Serious Call*, he quoted at length from the story of the great judgment in Matthew 25:31-46 to illustrate how far short the Christians of his day were from acting like those sheep who are blessed because they have ministered to the needy.[7]

Some other Scriptures that advocates of simplicity have used include the following:

> Therefore, I tell you, do not worry about your life, what you will eat or what you will drink, or about your body, what you will wear. Is not life more than food, and the body more than clothing? (Matt 6:25)

> Woe to you who are rich, for you have received your consolation. (Luke 6:24)

> Come now, you rich people, weep and wail for the miseries that are coming to you. Your riches have rotted, and your clothes are moth-eaten. Your gold and silver have rusted, and their rust will be evidence against you, and it will eat your flesh like fire. You have laid up treasure for the last days. . . . You have lived on the earth in luxury and in pleasure; you have fattened your hearts in a day of slaughter. (Jas 5:1-3, 5)

> Thieves must give up stealing; rather let them labor and work honestly with their own hands, *so as to have something to share with the needy.* (Eph 4:28, italics added)

In his book on spiritual disciplines, Richard Foster outlines ten outward expressions of simplicity.[8] While all ten are valuable, I wish to emphasize three of them.

We should buy things for their usefulness rather than their status. Law emphasized this in terms of clothing. Today we would want to add things such as furniture and cars. If we feel compelled to match our neighbors and friends in terms of fashion and brand name, perhaps we need to move to a new neighborhood! Foster quotes with approval these lines from John Wesley: "As . . . for apparel, I buy the most lasting and, in general, the plainest I can. I buy no furniture but what is necessary and cheap."[9]

Foster also suggested developing a habit of giving things away. Human beings can easily become pack rats. We hate to part with anything. Our closets, drawers, attics, and basements are full of accumulated things. The fact is, many of us could give away half of what we have and not experience any real deprivation. Of course, we could also sell the same and give the proceeds to the needy.

The third suggestion is that we resist the call to buy the most modern devices. Resist those advertisers who make us feel guilty for owning a ten-year-old car or a computer that cannot do the latest gyrations some whiz has devised. Isn't it just possible we could get by without a CD player that plays ten CDs without having to be reprogammed? Remember that the purpose of earning money, according to Paul, is not to satisfy our desire to buy the latest gadget, but to be able to help the needy.

Of the six disciplines discussed in this volume—confession, Holy Communion, service, prayer, study, and simplicity—simplicity may be the most difficult for Western Christians to practice. Certainly my own guilt level rises more as I reflect on this one than on the others. I suspect I am not alone. In America, we live in an economic system that depends on convincing us to buy more and more. When we quit buying, the financial markets shudder. I am not advocating a non-capitalistic economic system, but it has become increasingly clear to me that, as Christians, we must swim against the stream when it comes to deciding how we should use our money.

A story is told in Luke 9 of someone who said to Jesus, "I will follow you wherever you go." Jesus said to him, "Foxes have holes, and birds of the air have nests; but the Son of Man has nowhere to lay his head" (vv. 57, 58). Whatever else this passage may mean, it is clear that those who would truly follow Jesus are unlikely to amass the things that impress people of the world. A disciple will practice the discipline of simplicity, for such was the lifestyle of Jesus.

Evelyn Underhill, from whose writings I have learned much, wrote eloquently on this matter of simplicity.

> Consider that wonderful world of life in which you are placed, and observe that its great rhythms of birth, growth and death—all things that really matter—are not in your control. That unhurried process will go forward in its stately beauty, little affected by your anxious fuss. Find out, then, where your treasure really is. Discern substance from accident. Don't confuse your meals with your life, and your clothes with your body. Don't lose your head over what perishes. Nearly everything does perish: so face the facts, don't rush after the transient and unreal. Maintain your soul in tranquil dependence on God; don't worry; don't mistake what you possess for what you are. Accumulating things is useless. Both mental and material avarice are merely silly in view of the dread facts of life and death. The White Knight would have done better had he left his luggage at home. The simpler your house, the easier it will be to run. The fewer the things and the people you "simply must have," the nearer you will be to the ideal of happiness—"as having nothing, to possess all."[10]

Lectio Divina

> *Someone in the crowd said to him, "Teacher, tell my brother to divide the family inheritance with me." But he said to him, "Friend, who set me to be a judge or arbitrator over you?" And he said to them, "Take care! Be on your guard against all kinds of greed; for one's life does not consist in the abundance of possessions." Then he told them a parable: "The land of a rich man produced abundantly. And he thought to himself, 'What should I do, for I have no place to store my crops?' Then he said, 'I will do this: I will pull down my barns and build larger ones, and there I will store all my grain and my goods. And I will say to my soul, "Soul, you have ample goods laid up for many years; relax, eat, drink, be merry." But God said to him, 'You fool! This very night*

your life is being demanded of you. And the things you have pre-pared, whose will they be?' So it is with those who store up treasures for themselves but are not rich toward God." (Luke 12:13-21)

Examen

To begin to simplify your life, make a list of things you own that you no longer use. Give them away, or sell them and donate the money to a worthy cause.

Prayer

O God, we affirm that every good and perfect gift comes down from heaven—from you who are full of light. Thank you for the sunlight, the flowing stream, the snow-covered mountains. Thank you for cats and dogs, birds and fish. Thank you for family and friends. Thank you for the blessings of our lives. We affirm that a simple life need not be an empty one. We rejoice that our lives may be full of God and God's blessings. Help us, O gracious God, to become more like you. May we be givers rather than hoarders. Make our hearts wide with divine generosity. All of this we pray in the name of Jesus, the one who, though he possessed the prerog-atives of God, emptied himself and lived and died in service of God and humanity. Amen.

Notes

[1]William Law, *A Serious Call to a Devout and Holy Life*, in *William Law: A Serious Call to a Devout and Holy Life [and] The Spirit of Love*, edited by Paul G. Stanwood (New York: Paulist Press, 1978) 112.

[2]Ibid., 96-97.

[3]Ibid., 99.

[4]Ibid., 113-14.

[5]Ibid., 144.

[6]A. Keith Walker, *William Law: His Life and Thought* (London: S.P.C.K., 1973) 168-75.

[7]Law, *Serious Call*, 99-100.

[8]Richard Foster, *Celebration of Discipline: The Path to Spiritual Growth* (New York: HarperCollins, 1978; rev. ed. 1988) 90-95.

[9]Ibid., 90.

[10]Bob and Michael W. Benson, *Disciplines for the Inner Life* (Nashville: Thomas Nelson, rev. ed. 1989) 294.

ᴄꙅ5ᴄꙅ

MEDITATIONS

Day One

All Salvation is, and can be nothing else, but the Manifestation of the Life of God in the Soul[1]

Selah

Although William Law is well known for his emphasis on outward works and habits, he never tired of insisting that true religion was the inner experience of the living God. In a work that preceded *A Serious Call*, he wrote,

> We are true Members of the Kingdom of God, when the Kingdom of God is within us, when the Spirit of Religion is the Spirit of our Lives, when seated in our Hearts, it diffuses itself into all our Motions, when we are wise by its Wisdom, sober by its Sobriety, and humble by its Humility; when it is the Principle of all our Thoughts and Desires, the Spring of all our Hopes and Fears; when we like and dislike, seek and avoid, mourn and rejoice, as becomes those who are born again of God. Now this is the Work of the Holy Spirit in our Hearts, to give us a *new Understanding, a new Judgment, Temper, Taste, and Relish, new Desires and new Hopes and Fears.*[2]

Later he wrote: "All our Salvation consists in the *Manifestation of the Nature, Life, and Spirit of Jesus Christ, in our inward new Man.* This alone is Christian Redemption."[3]

The Church has developed many forms: Roman Catholic solemnity before Mass, Orthodox icons drawing the faithful to meditation, the quiet of a Quaker meeting, the shouts of a Pentecostal revival, Episcopal liturgy, Baptist spontaneity. But within all of this wonderful variety are those who remind us that true religion is indeed the life of God in the human soul.

Lectio Divina

But when the fullness of time had come, God sent his Son, born of a woman, born under the law, in order to redeem those who were under the law, so that we might receive adoption as children. And because you are children, God has sent the Spirit of his Son into our hearts, crying, "Abba! Father!" (Gal 4:4-6)

Examen

It is possible to say a pray without speaking to God. It is possible to serve others without intending to serve God. It is possible to live simply, but without peace, and to study without learning truth. Pray that God will renew your inner person so that the disciplines and all of your life will be directed by the spirit of Christ.

Prayer

Father, Son, and Holy Spirit, dwell in me. I open my heart anew to you. Fill me with your presence. Guide me with the inner light of your love. Draw me to yourself. I am bold to pray this because I believe it is your will. Amen.

Day Two

*Wherever thou goest, whatever thou dost, at Home, or Abroad,
in the Field, or at church, do all in a Desire of Union with Christ,
in Imitation of his Tempers and Inclinations, and look upon all as
Nothing, but that which exercises, and increases the Spirit and
Life of Christ in thy Soul. From Morning to Night keep Jesus in
thy Heart, long for Nothing, desire Nothing, hope for Nothing,
but to have all that is within Thee changed into the Spirit and
Temper of the Holy Jesus. Let this be thy Christianity, thy Church,
and thy Religion.*[4]

Selah

In those wild and strange 60s, the Jesus People emerged out of the
hippie culture. I don't know what William Law would have made
of them, but I do know that some were sincere in their desire to follow
and be like their Jesus.

We don't have to be exactly like those Jesus lovers of thirty years
ago, but if we are lovers of Jesus today, we too will be different. It is
simply impossible to truly love Jesus and be like those who do not.

Before there was William Law, there was another lover of Jesus
named Richard Rolle. He wrote:

> Fix this name "Jesus" so firmly in your heart that it never leaves your
> thought. And when you speak to him using your customary name
> "Jesu," in your ear it will be joy, in your mouth honey, and in your
> heart melody, because it will seem joy to you to hear that name
> being pronounced, sweetness to speak it, cheer and singing to think
> it. . . . Think of the name "Jesu" continually and cling to it
> devotedly.[5]

Lectio Divina

*Yet whatever gains I had, these I have come to regard as loss
because of Christ. More than that, I regard everything as loss
because of the surpassing value of knowing Christ Jesus my Lord.*

For his sake I have suffered the loss of all things, and I regard them as rubbish, in order that I may gain Christ and be found in him, not having a righteousness of my own that comes from the law, but one that comes through faith in Christ, the righteousness from God based on faith. I want to know Christ and the power of his resurrection and the sharing of his sufferings by becoming like him in death. (Phil 3:7-10)

Examen

Do you love Jesus? Close your eyes and say or sing the words of the old chorus, "Jesus in the morning, Jesus in the noon time, Jesus when the sun goes down." Repeat it until you feel the reality of the words welling up within you.

Prayer

Jesus, my everlasting love, inflame my soul until I love God so much that nothing burns in me but his desires. Good Jesus, shed yourself into the innermost depths of my soul. Come into my heart, and fill it with your sweetness. Moisten my mind with your sweet love's hot wine so that I forget all unhappiness and ridiculous dreams. Let me be happy only in your presence in me and rejoice only in Jesus, my God. From now on, sweetest Lord, do not leave me. Stay with me wholeheartedly in all your sweetness, for my only comfort is your presence, and only your absence can make me sorrowful. Amen.[6]

Day Three

The light of God cannot arise or be found in you by any art or contrivance of yours.[7]

Selah

William Law is justly famous for his advocacy of rules and habits for the Christian life. His most well-known work, *A Serious Call to a Devout and Holy Life,* is filled with advice about structuring our lives so they might be pleasing to God.

In *The Spirit of Love*, however, from which the quote for day one is taken, a different Law seems to be writing. Indeed, a few pages before those lines, Theogenes asks Theophilus (who represents Law) about rules, methods, and practices that will help us to overcome Satan and our own sinful nature. His response? "There is no need of a number of practices or methods in this matter."[8]

Law was not really arguing against his earlier works. He was writing truth early and late. Rules and methods do assist us as we grow in the Christian life. That is the premise of the disciplines. But the disciplines or rules without a right intention or the grace of God are not only worthless, they are dangerous.

Specific practices and religious habits are the accidents of our faith, not the essence. They are the body of our religious life, not the spirit. In the end we must depend on God and not the "art and contrivance" of our religious practices.

Lectio Divina

The woman said to him, "Sir, I see that you are a prophet. Our ancestors worshiped on this mountain, but you say that the place where people must worship is in Jerusalem." Jesus said to her, "Woman, believe me, the hour is coming when you will worship the Father neither on this mountain nor in Jerusalem. You worship what you do not know; we worship what we know, for salvation is from the Jews. But the hour is coming, and is now

87

here, when the true worshipers will worship the Father in spirit and truth, for the Father seeks such as these to worship him. God is spirit, and those who worship him must worship him in spirit and truth." (John 4:19-24)

Examen

My tendency during times of spiritual dryness is either to redouble my efforts in terms of my current practices and disciplines or disheartedly give up particular practices and disciplines. A frantic search for new methods usually follows any giving up of old ones. What are your tendencies?

I think there is a better way. Rather than tense up or give up, maybe I should rest up. That is, be still and wait for God to lead me on or out or in. Now if I can just remember that when I stumble into the next desert!

Prayer

God of our fathers, God of our mothers, I rejoice that they affirmed your grace in their lives. I rejoice that you fed them and led them. I need you to help me, Lord. I am willing to live a disciplined life. I am ready to adopt new methods or lay aside old techniques. I am prepared to walk the roads others have trod or to blaze new trails. But I know that whatever I do is worthless unless it is grounded in and surrounded by and infused with your grace. I want to be like Christ. Grow me, Lord. Amen.

Day Four

I join therefore in the public Assemblies, not because of the Purity of Perfection of that which is done, or to be found there, but because of that which is meant and intended by them: They mean the holy, public Worship of God; they mean the Edification of Christians; they are of great Use to many People; they keep the World from a total Forgetfulness of God; they help the Ignorant and Letterless to such a Knowledge of God, and the Scriptures, as they would not have without them.[9]

Law struggled with the church of his day. He had disagreements with the local priests. In spite of this, he refused to desert the church. I can relate to this commitment to the church.

Although they were not and are not perfect, I am thankful for the churches of my life. From Albertville, Alabama, to El Sobrante, California, to Bangkok, Thailand, to Buffalo, New York, to New Orleans, Louisiana, I have found churches in which I can worship, be edified, and serve.

Let us love the church because it is a blessing to many. Let us love the church because it is loved by Jesus. Let us love the church because, in spite of the imperfections we bring to it, it brings people to God and God to people.

Lectio Divina

To the angel of the church in Ephesus write: These are the words of him who holds the seven stars in his right hand, who walks among the seven golden lampstands: I know your works, your toil and your patient endurance. I know that you cannot tolerate evildoers; you have tested those who claim to be apostles but are not, and have found them to be false. I also know that you are enduring patiently and bearing up for the sake of my name, and that you have not grown weary. But I have this against you, that you have abandoned the love you had at first. Remember then from what you have fallen; repent, and do the works you did at first. If not,

I will come to you and remove your lampstand from its place, unless you repent. Yet this is to your credit: you hate the works of the Nicolaitans, which I also hate. Let anyone who has an ear listen to what the spirit is saying to the churches. To everyone who conquers, I will give permission to eat from the tree of life that is in the paradise of God. (Rev 2:1-7)

Examen

In a real sense, we who are believers are the church. When we repent, we repent for the church. Perhaps today would be a good time to examine our lives to see if we have left the love we had at first.

Prayer

I thank you triune God for the church. It is the people of God and the body of Christ. The Spirit binds the people together and enlivens the Body. Help me to never hinder the work of your Spirit. Help me to promote unity and godliness in the church. I confess that sometimes one or the other overwhelms my perspective. Give me balance in my life, a balance that will contribute to a church that is always pleasing to you. Amen.

Day Five

This Spirit of Faith, which not here, or there, or now and then, but everywhere, and in all Things, looks up to God alone, trusts solely in him, depends absolutely upon him, expects all from him, and does all it does for him, is the utmost Perfection of Piety in this Life.[10]

Selah

Years ago in a California church meeting, one of the young people opined that it was possible to be too religious. In the context of his life and those present circumstances, he did not mean, as some might suppose today, that religion can get in the way of spirituality. No, he meant that there was more to life than religion and spirituality. I think William Law would have taken issue with the boy. For him, faith was the orientation of every area of his life to God. While there is more to life than the structures of religious practice, God is what life is all about. And faith is the only appropriate response.

Lectio Divina

Now faith is the assurance of things hoped for, the conviction of things not seen. Indeed, by faith our ancestors received approval. . . . By faith Able offered to God a more acceptable sacrifice than Cain's. . . . By faith Noah, warned by God about events as yet unseen, respected the warning and built an ark to save his household; . . . By faith Abraham obeyed when he was called to set out for a place that he was to receive as an inheritance; and he set out, not knowing where he was going. . . . By faith Moses, when he was grown up, refused to be called a son of Pharaoh's daughter, choosing rather to share ill-treatment with the people of God than to enjoy the fleeting pleasures of sin. . . . By faith the people passed through the Red Sea as if it were dry land, . . . By faith Rahab the prostitute did not perish with those who were disobedient, because she had received spies in peace. (Heb 11:1-2, 4, 7-8, 24-25, 29, 31)

Examen

Someone once said that to believe in the righteousness of God meant to believe that God will do the right thing. Choose one of the persons of faith from Hebrews 11 and meditate on that life. Picture the circumstances. Feel the person's faith. For some it would certainly have been fear-tinged, looking into a cloudy future. Then reaffirm your own faith in a righteous God.

Prayer

God of Abel, God of Abraham and Sarah, God of Rahab, call forth faith in me. May the sacrifices of my life be acceptable to you. Help me to walk with faith even those roads whose ends I cannot see. Give me the courage to serve you when all around me are those who oppose your will. I trust you Lord. Help me to trust you more. In the name of Jesus who surrendered his life into your life-giving hands. Amen.

Day Six

The best way of showing true zeal is to make little things the occasions of great piety.[11]

Selah

Blessing the children, touching a leper, talking to a woman at a well, eating with friends, washing dirty feet—the "little things" . . . Sure Jesus did the "big things" well. He drove out demons, gave sight to the blind, cast out the money-changers in the temple, died for the sin of the world, rose from the grave. But the little things did not escape his notice either.

Life is made up of very few big events, but countless little ones. It seems a waste of time to prepare for the momentous times while ignoring the moments, pregnant with opportunity, that come each day.

Lectio Divina

When the Son of Man comes in his glory, and all the angels with him, then he will sit on the throne of his glory. All the nations will be gathered before him, and he will separate people one from another as a shepherd separates the sheep from the goats, and he will put the sheep at his right hand and the goats at the left. Then the king will say to those at his right hand, "come, you that are blessed by my Father, inherit the kingdom prepared for you from the foundation of the world; for I was hungry and you gave me food, I was thirsty and you gave me something to drink, I was a stranger and you welcomed me, I was naked and you gave me clothing, I was sick and you took care of me, I was in prison and you visited me." The righteous will answer him, "Lord, when was it that we saw you hungry and gave you food, or thirsty and gave you something to drink? And when was it that we saw you a stranger and welcomed you, or naked and gave you clothing? And when was it that we saw you sick or in prison and visited you?" And the king will answer them, "Truly I tell you, just as you

93

did it to one of the least of these who are members of my family,
you did it to me." (Matt 25:31-40)

Examen

The mind is an amazing thing. It can filter out thousands of pieces of
data that are constantly bombarding it. Without this ability, we would
be helpless. Concentration on any one item would be impossible.
However, this filtering process has one drawback. Sometimes we don't
notice the opportunities of service in the little things around us. Pray
that today you will notice and serve.

Prayer

O Lord Jesus Christ, you did not come to the world to be served,
but also surely not to be admired or in that sense to be worshiped.
You were the way and the truth, and it was followers only that you
demanded. Arouse us therefore if we have dozed away into this
delusion; save us from the error of wishing to admire you instead
of being willing to follow you and to resemble you. For your sake
and the sake of the world. Amen.[12]

Day Seven

If you will here stop and ask yourself why you are not as pious as the primitive Christians were, your own heart will tell you that it is neither through ignorance nor inability, but purely because you never thoroughly intended it.[13]

Selah

This one sentence from Law's *Serious Call* has haunted me for twenty years. It is the one quote from Law I have used over and over again in sermons and lectures. I know the "primitive Christians" were in fact a mixed lot. Some were disciplined and holy. Others were worldly. Some exuded love and compassion. A bitter spirit manifested itself in others. Such knowledge, however, does not relieve my burden.

Why am I not as pure and holy as I know I should be? Can I blame it on God? God forbid. If I am not what I should be, it is because, as Law said, my intention is lacking. What can I do?

I remember as a child hearing an evangelist encouraging people to walk the aisle in decisions for Christ. He said if we would make the first step, we would find Christ walking down the aisle with us. Perhaps it is the same with our intentions toward holiness. Let us voice them to God, asking the one who loves us to strengthen them until, like the best of the early Christians, we are devout and holy. Like the believing unbelieving father in the Gospels, let us pray, "I intend to live a life of holiness, help my disinclination to do so."

Lectio Divina

In the presence of God and of Christ Jesus, who is to judge the living and the dead, and in view of his appearing and his kingdom, I solemnly urge you: proclaim the message; be persistent whether the time is favorable or unfavorable; convince, rebuke, and encourage, with the utmost patience in teaching. For the time is coming when people will not put up with sound doctrine, but having itching ears, they will accumulate for themselves teachers to suit their own desires, and will turn away from listening to the truth and wander away to myths. As for you, always be sober, endure suffering, do the work of an evangelist, carry out your ministry fully.

As for me, I am already being poured out as a libation, and the time of my departure has come. I have fought the good fight, I have finished the race, I have kept the faith. From now on there is reserved for me the crown of righteousness, which the Lord, the righteous judge, will give me on that day, and not only to me but also to all who have longed for his appearing. (2 Tim 4:1-8)

Examen

Today make a list of three or four things you want more than any other. Be as honest as your heart will let you. Pray over the list, asking God to help you to want what is right, to intend what is good.

Prayer

Heavenly Father, I confess my imperfections and my sins. I have fallen short of your glory. I have fallen short of Paul's glory. I have fallen short of the glory of many faithful believers in my own day. Forgive me and make me whole. Amen.

Notes

[1] William Law, *The Spirit of Love* (London: G. Robertson and J. Roberts, 1752) 45, in *The Works of the Reverend William Law*, vol. 8 (New York: Hildesheim, 1974).

[2] William Law, *A Practical Treatise upon Christian Perfection* (London: William and John Innys, 1726) 142, in *The Works of the Reverend William Law*, vol. 3 (New York: Hildesheim, 1974).

[3] William Law, *The Spirit of Prayer; or, The Soul Rising out of the Vanity of Time, into the Riches of Eternity* (London: M. Richardson, 1749) 24, in *The Works of the Reverend William Law*, vol. 7 (New York: Hildesheim, 1974).

[4] Ibid., 24.

[5] Quoted in Harvey Egan, *An Anthology of Christian Mysticism* (Collegeville MN: Liturgical Press) 309.

[6] This prayer is a modernized and shortened form of a prayer by Richard Rolle from "The Love of God," in *The Cell of Self-Knowledge: Early English Mystical Treatises by Margery Kempe and Others* (New York: Crossroad, 1981) 113.

[7] William Law, *The Spirit of Love* in *William Law: A Serious Call to a Devout and Holy Life [and] The Spirit of Love*, edited by Paul G. Stanwood (New York: Paulist Press, 1978) 497.

[8] Ibid., 485.

[9] William Law, *A Collection of Letters on the Most Interesting and Important Subjects, and on Several Occasions* (London: J. Richardson, 1760) 117-18, in *The Works of the Reverend William Law*, vol. 9 (New York: Hildesheim, 1974).

[10] Ibid., 121.

[11] William Law, *A Serious Call to a Devout and Holy Life* in *William Law: A Serious Call to a Devout and Holy Life [and] The Spirit of Love*, edited by Paul G. Stanwood (New York: Paulist Press, 1978) 327.

[12] This prayer was adapted from Søren Kierkegaard, *The Prayers of Kierkegaard*, edited by Perry D. LeFevre (Chicago: University of Chicago Press) 96.

[13] William Law, *Serious Call*, 57.

❧ REFLECTIONS ON CATHERINE ❧